On Eagle Wings

VOLUME VII in the TRUETT MEMORIAL SERIES

ON EAGLE WINGS

by

GEORGE W. TRUETT, D.D., LL.D.

Compiled and Edited by
Powhatan W. James, Th.D., D.D.

BAKER BOOK HOUSE
Grand Rapids, Michigan

PHOTOLITHOPRINTED BY CUSHING - MALLOY, INC.
ANN ARBOR, MICHIGAN, UNITED STATES OF AMERICA
1973

DEDICATION

This and other volumes
of sermons and addresses
in this series by Dr. George W. Truett
are dedicated to
his beloved
First Baptist Church, Dallas, Texas,
where most of them
were delivered

F O R E W O R D

What a man believes is important because belief has much to do with determining character and conduct.

George W. Truett, with Paul, believed that "All scripture is given by inspiration of God, and is profitable for doctrine, for reproof, for correction, for instruction in righteousness: that the man of God may be perfect, thoroughly furnished unto all good works." Because he so believed he frequently preached on Old Testament themes — almost as often as on New Testament themes.

This volume, number VII in the *Truett Memorial Series*, presents fourteen Old Testament sermons delivered at the First Baptist Church, Dallas, Texas, of which he was pastor for forty-seven years.

Because this man of God did "wait upon the Lord" and thereby received the strength that enabled him so often to mount as on eagle wings; to run, and not be weary; to walk, and not faint, we have decided to let this volume be entitled *On Eagle Wings*.

Powhatan W. James

5105 Live Oak St.,
Dallas, Texas

CONTENTS

CHAPTER I

On Eagle Wings

C H A P T E R   I

On Eagle Wings

~~~~~~

> *They shall mount up with wings as eagles.*
> —Isaiah 40:31

On THIS our forty-first anniversary together as pastor and people, I desire to bring to your remembrance a fortifying promise for the days ahead. It is found in the last words of the fortieth chapter of Isaiah:

> *But they that wait upon the Lord shall renew their strength; they shall mount up with wings as eagles; they shall run, and not be weary; they shall walk, and not faint.*

It would be difficult to find, even in the Bible, another chapter more lofty in thought or eloquent in speech than this chapter of Isaiah. Many of the noblest minds through the centuries have been profoundly influenced by it.

Handel's majestic oratorio, *The Messiah,* owes much of its inspiration to this fortieth chapter of Isaiah. Martin Luther pored over it again and again in the fortress at Salzburg. Oliver Cromwell frequently turned to it for refreshment and inspiration in the days when he was terribly discouraged. Daniel Webster read this chapter when defeat and disappointment seemed inevitable, and he said that every time he read it he found new hope and new heart. Carlyle, Tennyson and Wordsworth all recorded their indebtedness to this great chapter from the pen of the great prophet of the eighth century, B. C.

In the midst of this chapter Isaiah tells of the gentleness and the greatness of God. He pictures Him as a Shepherd looking after His flock with all diligence and devotion. He pictures Him as carrying the little lamb in His arms, tenderly pressed against His great bosom; and as gently leading those that are with young.

But God is great as well as gentle. He can hold the waters of the oceans in the hollow of His hand. He can weigh the mighty mountains in scales and the hills in a balance. Compared with His greatness the nations are as a drop of water in a bucket; they are counted by Him as less than nothing, as a mere speck of dust on His eternal scales.

In contrast with God's greatness, the prophet points out our littleness, weakness and frailty. He reminds us that our boasted strength becomes enervated, our minds are weakened, our fancied powers are reduced and depleted. Even the young men shall faint and resilient youth shall become weary. In other words, even at his best, the natural man, apart from God, is doomed to failure and defeat.

But Isaiah proclaims an entirely different story concerning those who trust in God. The declaration is: "They that wait upon the Lord shall renew their strength; they shall mount up with wings as eagles; they shall run, and not be weary; they shall walk, and not faint."

There are great lessons in this fortifying promise. May we, with the help of the Holy Spirit, find some of them today.

First of all, we are reminded here that if we are to have this needed strength we are to *wait upon the Lord*. And what does this *waiting* mean? It means one clear, definite thing — that we are to put our trust in Him. When we come to the New Testament, it talks about belief. "Believe on the Lord Jesus Christ and thou shalt be saved." We who put our trust in the Lord shall be saved; waiting upon the Lord means that. "Wait then always upon the Lord, oh my soul," said the Psalmist, and then he added, "for my expectation is from Him."

We are to put our trust in a *person*. "Wait thou upon the Lord." A *person*. When the sailor read about the Lord holding the seas in the hollow of His hand, being a Christian sailor, he said, "Very well; if I go down in the sea, I will be in the hollow of God's hand, and will be saved, so I will not worry at all." "He shall not be afraid of evil tidings; his heart is fixed, trusting in the Lord." We are to wait upon a person.

Our trust is to be put in a person as definitely as a sick man turns his troubled body over to the capable doctor; as definitely as a man troubled with all of the worries of his trial in court turns his case over to the competent advocate; as definitely as the troubled pupil in the school brings him-self to the teacher for his lesson help. We are to wait upon the Lord by committing ourselves unto Him. "Commit thy way unto the Lord; trust also in Him and He shall bring it to pass." Waiting upon a person. Oh, in this day when we hear so much about forms and ceremonies and conventions and creeds, ritualism and ecclesiasticisms, we are in constant peril of losing sight of the supreme truth that our hope and our help for time and eternity are in a person, *in one person*. We are to wait upon the Lord.

When the little girl lost her mother — her father had al-ready gone — and there was nothing to do but to put her in the orphans' home, they found her evening after evening quietly sobbing to herself, and one day one of the teachers said to her, "Why are you crying?"

She replied, "I want somebody to cry to. If my mamma were here, I could cry to her, but she is gone. I want somebody to cry to." She wanted somebody to lean on; somebody to cry to.

All through the Bible, there is the union of the Divine and the human in reference to God and man. There is a union of the Divine and the human in these blessings. When the Israelites came to the Red Sea and saw the water in front of them and they were pressed by the hosts of Pharaoh at their rear, they seemed done for. But the Lord said unto Moses: "Speak unto the children of Israel that they go forward. Lift thou up thy rod, and stretch out thine hand over the sea and divide it." Then the Lord opened the way through the sea for his people, to safety.

There is the union of the Divine and the human in that happy hour yonder at the wedding feast in Cana, when the water was turned into wine, as the story is told in the Gospels. The word of Jesus was given to the servants: "Fill the water pots with water and draw out and bear to the governor of the feast." Jesus had turned the water into wine, for the comfort and convenience of the guests.

Again when Lazarus lay dead and his two broken-hearted sisters stood beside the grave and the people came around to sympathize with them, Jesus said: "Take away the stone." He could have taken away the stone by a word, but that is not His method. He uses humanity, for He needs humanity to facilitate His work. "Take away the stone," and Lazarus came forth with the grave clothes still about him. Jesus said, "Remove the grave clothes." He could have removed them with a command, but what you and I can do He wants us to do. Let us never forget that.

The motto over a hospital gate in Scotland has the right idea. Here it is: "We dress his wounds; God heals him." Certainly we can dress each other's wounds; we can bring poultices and bandages and medicine; we can dress the wounds, but that is about as far as we can go. God heals us. God makes use of human resources, of human assets, human power, and even though we have just one talent, it is to be laid on His altar unreservedly, unhesitatingly, and He will add His blessing. Our "waiting upon the Lord" means to trust Him, as we seek to do His will according to His own Word.

Here, then, a blessing is promised us if we wait upon the Lord. I would like for us to notice this blessing that is promised. What will follow? What reward will come? Mark it: "They that wait upon the Lord shall renew their strength; they shall mount up with wings as eagles; they

shall run, and not be weary; they shall walk, and not faint."
Marvelous catalog of blessings, is it not? Let us look at this
promise a little more carefully.

First of all, they that wait upon the Lord shall *renew their
strength*. Now, that is what you and I, my dear friends,
need all along this busy way, in the humdrum day's work
that comes to us, renewal of strength. They that wait upon
the Lord shall renew their strength. The batteries of their
lives shall be recharged with divine power, if they patiently
and trustfully wait upon the Lord. Glorious promise.
Blessed reward is this.

After you have come to the end of your own strength and
spent your last powers, you can come with unreserved commitment to the Lord and say, "Build Thou me up; put
power again within me; renew my strength that I may be
strong to do Thy will to the end of the earthly day." You
can plead this promise, provided you truly wait upon the
Lord.

Now, we should remember that we are to go one day at
a time. God does not promise us strength for two days at
a time, or two weeks, or a year. Strength for one day at a
time. One of the most beautiful promises in all the Bible
is this one: "As thy days, so shall thy strength be." He
does not say: "as thy years," or "as thy months," or "as thy
weeks," but "as thy days," one day at a time. He just offers
us strength for one day at a time, and we are to let it go
at that and live at our maximum that one day. Let us live
this one day at our best by witnessing and working for the
Divine Saviour and Lord, one day at a time.

We walk by faith, not by sight. We do not know what is
ahead. If we knew the black Fridays that may be out there
ahead, our hearts would sink within us. We would be unfitted for the mighty demands upon us right now, if we
knew of the separations, of the desolating break-ups in our
homes and in our lives out there ahead. We must wait until
we get there and His grace will be ample, surely. He hides

from us our successes. If we knew that out yonder were great chapters of success, we would be largely unfitted to go on and fulfill the demands upon us today. He hides these things from us.

They tell us that when Rudyard Kipling came over to this country to visit he brought with him his little daughter, Josephine, and that on the ship as they came over, they had great joy in each other's companionship — the tiny little girl, Josephine, and the father — and their joy was so great that the passengers took notice of them playing together on the deck of the ship.

They had a delightful time together, but when they got over here she was taken very ill, and soon died. In a few days the father became seriously sick and kept calling, ill though he was: "Jo, where is Jo? Why does she not come? Where is little Jo?" Little Jo was sleeping under the snow and the ice. Now what a mercy that while the father and the child played together on the ship and had such delight in each other, what a mercy that he did not know that two or three weeks later little Jo would be taken from him, never to be with him again on this earth. What a mercy. One day at a time are we to live.

This may be our last day. Then let us live it at our highest. Let us be more humble, more devoted today, and live at our maximum for Christ. "They that wait upon the Lord shall renew their strength; they shall mount up with wings as eagles." He gives strength to those who wait upon Him. We shall "mount up with wings as eagles." How high the eagle flies. Higher and higher toward the sun, above the mountains and the storms and the clouds, higher and higher. They that wait upon the Lord shall renew their strength; they shall mount up with wings as eagles; they shall fly higher and higher and shall understand some of the great things of God in the secrecy He has for those who wait upon Him.

18

A glorious promise! Freely translated it means that as friends of our Lord, as children of God by faith in Christ, He would have us enter into our spiritual inheritance. Why should we play the role of the cringing servant when the Lord says: "Ye are children of mine," heirs of God, joint-heirs with Christ; now are we the sons of God. We know that when He shall appear, we shall be like Him and we shall see Him as He is. Joint-heirs with Christ. To as many as received Him was given the power and the privilege to be the children of God. Here, says this great prophet Isaiah, we are to enter more and more into the graciousness and fullness of our inheritance. We are to wait upon the Lord.

Do you remember when the prodigal son came home? He wanted to come home as a wretched, cringing servant, and he needed to come back that way. He had behaved miserably. He said: "I will go back to my father and I will tell him that I am no longer worthy to be called his Son, and all that I ask is to have a place as one of his hired servants." But when he returned, he was taken into his father's arms of love. He was still a son, although his steps had been wayward and his behavior wretched. He was still a son. "Bring the best robe for the son; kill the fatted calf; make a feast for him; put the ring on his finger. My son, who was lost, is found!" Oh, is it not glorious to be a son of God, a daughter of God? What an exaltation to wait upon the Lord!

Here we are, children of the King. Come into the presence of the King; enter into the joy of your Lord. Rejoice, and again I say, rejoice, if you love the Lord. While you are here in this world, live on the uplands with God. "They that wait upon the Lord shall renew their strength; they shall mount up with wings as eagles; they shall run and not be weary." That means that He promises us strength for the emergency hour, for the crisis hour, for the great demanding hours that come in life. "They shall run and not

19

be weary." He promises us strength for the great days, for the black Fridays, for the days of bereavement, for the great days of conquest, for the great days of duty and responsibility. Wait on the Lord, trust in Him, cling to Him, and when those days come you will be undergirded, the everlasting arms will be around you and underneath you. A great promise that!

Martin Luther learned two great truths, namely: "the just shall live by faith," and "we are saved by a person." We are not saved by a church, nor by a sacrament so-called, nor by a creed, a ceremony, nor a ritual. Men are saved by a person, by faith in that person, and that person is the victorious, redeeming Saviour. When Martin Luther found out those truths, he avowed them, profoundly, mightily, and he stood bravely unafraid and said: "Here I take my stand. I can do no other, so help me God." And when they warned him what would happen if he went to Wurttemberg, he said: "I will go and I will declare there what I have found to be true, if every tile on every roof in Wurttemberg were a devil." God sustained him.

God sustained John Bunyan there in Bedford jail for twelve years. He sustained Paul in his prison experiences. He is sustaining men in Europe and in Asia through all the bloody, terrible wars. He is sustaining His children mightily around the world today.

"They shall run, and not be weary; they shall walk, and not faint." Is that an anti-climax? Not at all. If we walk and keep on walking, it is sometimes harder than running and stopping for awhile. We are to *walk and not faint*. There is nothing spectacular about just walking. The Lord says, "If you will wait on Me, I will help you in the humdrum of life. I will help you in the daily routine of life, when there is the weariness of monotony. I will help you in the home, in the church, in domestic affairs, in spiritual affairs, in affairs of state, if you will wait on me." Now, this is the promise for us today. It is a promise for us tomorrow. It is a promise for us until we get to the journey's end. *Wait upon the Lord!*

Let us make this promise ours today. More definitely, more personally, more confidently than ever before, let us make this promise our own. Let us tell our Lord today on this anniversary Sunday, all of us — preacher, teacher, every church officer at every post in the church, the parents, the aged, the middle-aged, and the young men and maidens, the eager, blessed boys and girls — let us say to this fortifying Saviour and Lord: "Have Thine own way, whatever it is. I will say Yes! wherever Thou leadest, I am ready; whatever Thou preparest for me, I accept. Today will I wait upon Thee."

This is an hour of unreserved commitment and dedication for me, your pastor, a re-dedication of my all to the Lord.

I have told you before of the great English preacher, John Robertson, who went for months and months in his ministry without any tokens of blessing, without any souls being saved, and after awhile the thought seemed to rage in his mind that if he was God's divinely called preacher, surely he would have had tokens of His blessing on his ministry, if he were divinely chosen to this great work. Months went on, without any change, and one night he told his family not to disturb him for he wanted to be alone in his library. He tells us he got down on his face before God and said, "I thought Thou hadst called me to be a preacher, but I seem to have been mistaken for there have been no tokens, no signs of blessing on my ministry in a long time. Let me resign my commission, Lord Jesus, to Thee. Let me resign my commission and turn to the work of the lawyer, the teacher or the doctor. Let me resign my commission." And he said that he seemed to hear a small voice say, "No, John Robertson, do not resign your commission. Let me re-sign your commission for you." And John Robertson said, "He re-signed my commission that night."

21

Shall we resign our commissions dear Lord, or wilt Thou re-sign them for us and renew our strength that we may serve Thee more acceptably? May the preacher, the teachers, the deacons and the parents of this church all so wait upon the Lord, that tomorrow and all the days may be marked with a diligence and a devotion as victorious witnesses for Christ, the like of which we have never known before.

Do you want to follow Christ today? Are there Christians here today who ought to link their lives with Christ's people? Come, and welcome. It may be you have waited late and long. Come for your own sake, but more, for the sake of others, come. If there is a secret friend of Jesus here in this great press of people, come out into the open and confess Him today!

Are you here today saying: "I have waited late in life; I have hesitated"? How long are you to halt between two opinions? Come out on His side and say: "I am ready. I choose Christ's side." Jesus died for you. Follow Him. Trust Him, dear friend, trust Him! Can you not say:

> Have Thine own way, Lord!
> Have Thine own way!
> Thou art the potter;
> I am the clay.

Now, as we sing, tarrying reverently just a moment or two, who wants to follow Christ and come into the church? Come on today, saying: "I wait upon the Lord." Do you say for the first time: "I choose Him; I have decided for Him; I surrender to Him; I receive Him; I give my heart to Him"? Come, as we sing together now: "Have Thine own way, Lord."

CHAPTER II

A Worthy Offering

CHAPTER II

A Worthy Offering

~~~~~~

> *Neither will I offer burnt offerings*
> *unto the Lord my God of that which*
> *doth cost me nothing.*
> —II SAMUEL 24:24

THE text this morning directs our attention to an Old Testament incident that is deeply suggestive of the spirit which should direct our offering for missions today.

> *And King David said to Ornan the Jebusite: "Nay, but*
> *I will verily buy it for the full price; for I will not take*
> *that which is thine for the Lord, nor offer burnt offerings*
> *without cost."*

It is a pitiful sight to observe any man traveling the wrong road. He is just as certain to come to distress going down the wrong road, as that God lives. "Whatsoever a man soweth, that shall he also reap." If a man sets wrong standards in his family, God pity his descendants. If a man lifts up the wrong standards as a citizen, dragons of death will follow in the wake of those wrong standards.

It is a pitiful thing, thrice pitiful, for an old man to miss the right road, and the tragedy deepens when a good man who is old misses the right road. That was so in the case of King David, as suggested by our text. He was an elderly man, full of honor, king of a great people, and yet he went at that advanced age into a grievous sin to be followed by strong chastisement. It is a great mercy of God that chastisement does come to men when they go wrong. If they were not checked, if they were not called to the consideration of the highest things, if there were no changes in

25

their lives, they would go on, reckless, presumptuous, and forgetful of God.

What was David's sin in his old age which led him into such sore grief and chastisement? It was the sin of numbering the people. It was the sin of taking the census of the kingdoms of Israel and Judah. Wherein was there sin in that? The sin was in his spirit, the spirit of pride that prompted him to have that census taken. The spirit of boastfulness over the resources of his great country, the spirit that said: "I and my people can withstand all hostile invaders and I am going to have the people numbered, and then, when they are numbered, we shall see what an invincible host is ours, and we shall have victories on our every campaign."

The spirit was wrong in that proud old man. He left God out of his count, and when any man leaves God out of his count, trouble is coming for such man. When any nation dares leave God out of her count, that nation is marked for disaster. God is the ultimate of all wisdom and all authority, and if men or nations leave Him out of their calculations, there comes a day, retributive and terrible, in the wake of such neglect. David left God out of his count, for awhile. He trusted in horses and chariots. He trusted in armies of flesh. He forgot the high and holy One who inhabiteth eternity. He forgot that man's goings, if they are established, must be established of the Lord. He forgot, for a season, that man must be amenable to the authority of the King of heaven and earth. He turned to wholly material resources and for the time being failed to trust in God. Therefore he came to grievous defeat and sorrow. Let us never put our trust in mere carnal weapons and resources. Our hope is in the Lord who made heaven and earth. "Except the Lord build the house, they labor in vain that build it."

Our nation is doomed if she goes her way without God. She may pile up her armaments; she may drill her millions of men, but nations cannot with safety forget God, His counsel, His light and leading. It must be a matter of immeasurable satisfaction to every right-thinking man of this country that in this day of atheism and communism we still have presidents in the White House who bow their heads and call on God for light and leading in this incomparable day of history. We want a president who prays. We want a governor who prays. We want soldiers who pray. We want statesmen who pray.

Years ago, a statesman in the national congress, who imagined himself to be considerably somebody but who missed it quite as considerably, laughed at the Ten Commandments and the Golden Rule. Any nation that laughs at the Ten Commandments and the Golden Rule as a nation is already marked for deterioration and defeat.

Let a nation forget God and the day of her decline and deterioration comes on apace. Let us be warned by this Old Testament incident of a king and a people forgetting God. Let us note the sore chastisement that followed. Let us be warned by it with all simplicity and humiliation, morning, noon and night. Let us cling to God. He must "turn the battle back from the gate." He is humanity's one defense and hope and refuge.

When David discovered, fully, the awful blunder of his course, he was filled with penitence and grief. You will not find anything in literature more sublime than the grief poured out in the penitential psalm. If you wish to read a confession that bites and burns, read the fifty-first Psalm today. All through the Psalm David, without qualification, without self-justification, without palliation, without deception, said to God: "Have mercy upon me, O God, according to thy loving kindness; according unto the multitude of thy tender mercies, blot out my transgressions," and God always hears such a cry.

Is there some man here who has missed the road utterly? Is there some woman who has sinned until her sin stains her deepest soul — the saddest sight earth ever saw? Is she

27

here? Let her come, without any reservation, making full confession of the evil of her course, and turn from such course, utterly and forever, even this very day, and blessed be God, there is forgiveness, there is cleansing for that woman and that man today.

David confessed utterly the wrongness of his course and then God sent David's seer, whose name was Gad, and said to him: "Say to the king he can take his choice of the chastisement God is going to inflict." Great consideration that was of Jehovah, toward a man. "Tell King David he can take his choice of three chastisements; three years of famine, three months of war, or three days of pestilence which God will send." David said: "Let me not fall into the hand of man: I will take the three days of pestilence which God will send. I will take what He chooses."

You will remember that the pestilence raged for those three long days until seventy thousand brave men of Israel lay dead under the blight of that pestilence, and David's heart was poured out like water. He cried out to God saying: "I am to blame — let not these poor sheep about me, these people of mine, let not them suffer more — I am to blame; let Thy hand be on me and on my father's house. I am to blame." Then, again God said to Gad: "Tell him to build an altar and offer on that altar his offering, that the plague may be stayed."

So, David came to the threshing floor of Ornan, the Jebusite, who with his sons was threshing the wheat, and when David approached that chieftain, Ornan bowed himself in obeisance before the king who made known his wish. "I have come to buy the site of your threshing floor on which to build an altar, on which altar I am going to make an offering to God that the plague throughout Israel may be stayed. I am obeying God by the mouth of his servant in wanting to build an altar in this particular place. What will this place cost me?"

Ornan made quick reply to the king: "It is all yours. The site is yours; the threshing floor is yours, the wheat is yours. All is yours without any money and without any price."

Then it was that David made the sublime reply: "Nay, but I will verily buy it of thee at full price; I will not offer to the Lord my God of that which costs me nothing," and the trade was made. David paid Ornan six hundred shekels of gold for the site. The altar was reared, the offering was placed on the altar, the sacrifice came up before God and the plague throughout Israel was stayed. This historical incident of the Old Testament is profoundly suggestive. It points to the deeper lessons that were revealed in New Testament times when the light and glory of the cross should come to cover the world with mercy and blessedness.

Now, this text suggests a great lesson for us today. In this act of David he utterly repudiated all cheap service in the accomplishment of any high and worthy task. "I will verily buy it of thee and pay a full price. You cannot give it to me. I will not offer to the Lord my God an offering which costs me nothing. This offering that I am going to offer unto Jehovah God must be an offering that costs." In that memorable act, David forever repudiated all cheapness upon the part of men in their worship and service of the Lord.

In the mart of life about us, we have long since learned that the best things may be procured only by paying the full price for them. The full price must be paid in the market of life if the highest things are to be realized and achieved. All relations in life voice that same truth. Every relation in life magnifies that same fact. Take any relation, any realm; everywhere that truth is written as if in letters of fire that all men may read.

In the matter of education — whenever you see a college offering short courses in education, that is the school to which you should not send your child. Whenever you see a college where interlinears are allowed for students, there is a college fraudulent and its diplomas given to students are a fraud to them and to an unsuspecting public. A man is to be pitied for pretending to be what he is not. If a man essays himself to be something and is not, he is to be pitied, for the day will come when he will be utterly disillusioned and discredited. And the tests and revealings of life will uncover the dross in him and, sooner or later, he will stand as he is in the sight of men and in the sight of God. No man ought ever to pose one moment for something which he is not.

> *The heights by great men reached and kept*
> *Were not attained by sudden flight,*
> *But they, while their companions slept,*
> *Were toiling upward in the night.*

The students who achieve are the students who burn the midnight oil or who know how to conserve time, or the students who are methodical and conscientious in the great world of study. If men achieve the highest in any line, they must pay the highest price to reach such goal.

The business and professional men who have risen to worthy positions have paid the full price. They have risen early; they have toiled late. Men sometimes are lured by fantastic notions about men of genius. Men of genius generally are the most indefatigable toilers. One of the world's chief citizens who was supposed to be a genius was revealed by his biographer to be one who "could toil dreadfully."

One of the greatest chemists recently said in an interview that he gave sixteen hours a day to hard work. Edison, the "wizard" in electricity, was perhaps the world's most prodigious toiler of his age. Men in business and in professional life who come to the highest, pay the full price in the market of life. When you pass to the highest realm of all, the realm of character, there are tests and tribulations and winnowings and revealings in that realm. Men pay the price for the highest in the realm of character.

Somebody's blood went into the writing of every great book, the painting of every masterpiece, the building of every worthy institution for the help and healing and ennoblement of humanity. The best things come high, and someone must pay the full price for them.

Bunyan's *Pilgrim's Progress* stands next to the Holy Scriptures in the interest of man, but you must remember that for twelve long weary years Bunyan lay yonder in Bedford jail, by night and by day, confined and kept away from the loved ones of his heart. Milton sang his sonnets to the hill, but Milton came to blindness ere he could see the vision of *Paradise Lost.* When George Matheson, that brilliant, self-willed young Scotchman, was told by his physician that the dark shadow of blindness would be over him in only a few hours, he went aside, before the blindness did come, and wrote that immortal hymn:

> *Oh love that will not let me go,*
> *I rest my weary soul on Thee;*
> *I give Thee back the life I owe,*
> *That in Thine ocean depths its flow*
> *May richer, fuller be.*

These men paid the full price to gain immortality by penning their masterpieces.

The Anglo-Saxon word for "bless" is the word for blood, and if men bless the world, they must pour out their blood. Things that come easily, things that are bought cheaply, are of little worth. You do not wonder, therefore, that one of the world's great preachers often said: "When you cease to bleed, you cease to bless." In the market of life, we must pay the full price even unto blood, in reaching the highest in human achievement.

When Ornan, the Jebusite chieftain, proposed to David: "There is no cost for this site for your altar and there is no cost for the implements and these furnishings, the wood and the wheat that go into the arrangements for the altar," David was not pleased. Ornan proposed a way which, when followed, leads the world into the darkness of night. High things cost. Our offerings unto God call for love, self-denial, real sacrifice on our part.

The temptation all along is for us to accept the easy way, the velvet path proposed by Ornan. When we take that path we are dallying with death itself. It is not God's plan. It is not God's way. The scandal of Christianity this Sunday morning is that too many of Christ's people are treading the pathway that has in it no self-denial, no real sacrifice, no full dedication of themselves and their all unto Christ who purchased their salvation with his precious blood shed on Calvary's tree.

If we come to the highest, there must be shedding of blood. If you would save your life, you must lose it. You will lose it if you strive to save it. Now, that principle is written everywhere as plainly as if in capital letters of fire across the heavens above us today: "Those men who seek to save their lives must lose them." Let us not forget that. When England said to Gladstone: "Your time is out," he replied: "Very well, I will wait for the vindication that is coming tomorrow." And on the morrow he challenged England and her colonies and made them follow the road he pointed out. They knew then that he was a statesman.

Two business men taking the road side by side may come to very different ends. One is utterly self-centered: all life begins and ends with himself. He will come to defeat. The self-centered business or professional man is doomed to ultimate defeat. But the great, magnanimous man who can truly say: "I bring my calling, my daily work; I bring my bank or ranch or farm or store, I bring my vocation, I bring my all for the service of mankind" — the world will not let him die. Some day he will slip away and the flowers will be banked over his grave; but his spirit, his deeds, his blessed example will live on for generations. He will live on in human hearts. Both earth and heaven will sound forth his praise. If you would save your life, you must lose it by spending it for others. That is a law stated by Jesus for all human conduct.

When will we learn that the bane of life is to take the easy road? When will we learn that? This nation is now being jarred and shaken from the easy road. We have had velvet paths for a long time and cushioned chairs and a super-abundance of fine things to eat and to wear and to ride in. Now, with the world challenged by the most merciless enemy that ever challenged it in human history, we are seeing that to dally with the path of ease is to dally with sure death. We are learning that the way of ease is the way of ruin. History writes it for us and if we will open our eyes, there it is. The way of ease is the way of undoing and the way of death. The nations that have trodden the broad way of ease are the nations that have come to shameful disaster. The way of ease is the way of ruin.

God comes to His own people and reminds them: "Woe to them that are at ease in Zion." A church at ease is treading hard by the precipice. A church at ease is near the gates of destruction and ruin. A family at ease is in dire danger. I overheard this past week a certain man being discussed. The two men discussing him said: "Our trouble, our anguish about him is that life all begins and ends with self, and we tremble to think what he must face and suffer."

The way of ease is the way of death. Any man, no matter how powerful, who follows the path of ease, will fall. That will undo men when everything else fails. Hannibal, that marvelous soldier, had the people bowing before him as the grain bows before the passing breeze. Then one winter he rested in Capua and gave himself to selfish ease and to idle, sluggish ways, and that undid him. What the snows of the Alps could not do, and what the burning sands of Italy could not do, one season of selfish ease in Capua did. That season plunged the great soldier down into the deepest depths of shame and doom. The way of ease is the way of ruin. Surely that lesson is written for us very plainly today. As Christians, will we not see it? As preachers, will we not see it? As citizens, will we not see it? As humanitarians, will we not see that "when we cease to bleed we will cease to bless"? The offering we make to God and the world that has not cost us dearly is an offering practically without worth. Can we not see that? Oh, how failure comes to many Christians right there!

In this church, one of our devoted men went his way half-heartedly, lukewarmly in the Christian life for years and years. Then one day he said: "I have learned my lesson. I shut myself up a few days ago in a room and I made a true confession to God of the selfishness of my course. Then and there I utterly dedicated myself to God. Since I did that, I have lived days of heaven on earth, so wonderful has been my peace of mind and heart." For a number of years now, he has lived his life on as high a plane as any layman or preacher I have known.

And there is sitting here another man who, when the day of sickness came and his life hung on a threat, said: "Master, I have amounted to practically nothing so far. It seems to me, as my life hangs on just one threat, keeping me out of the grave, that my life is a vain thing. But if Thou wilt let me live, I will live for Thee the rest of the journey." Healing and health came and he is keeping his vow in a glorious way. He is spending himself in the service he is offering to humanity. When we cease to bleed we cease to bless. Now, we should lay it to heart that any cheap service which we offer to God or His church or to a needy world is a service that will not avail. This world struggle in which we are now engaged is spelling out this truth for us in letters as red as blood itself.

I read some time ago of a French mother who lost all five of her strong sons yonder in battle and when they brought her the message she said: "Leave me alone." All night long that French peasant woman looked out the window, her lips talking with Someone, talking with God, and when the gray of the early morning came, friends came and asked: "What can we say to you?" She replied: "Do not trouble about me: I thank God that I had five big boys to give for such a cause as this. Would God that I had five more to give for civilization and for human brotherhood." That is the spirit that will save civilization and humanity.

When another mother heard the sad story that the elder of her two sons had fallen on the soil of France, never to come home again, she in the gray of the morning after a night of anguish said to the younger one, the only one left: "Son, you must take your brother's place." That is the spirit which will save civilization and freedom for the earth.

A friend once told me of a letter written by a French mother to her only remaining son, in Canada. This is what she said: "My dear son. Your two brothers dedicated their lives to France and the cause of the allied countries and they brought me word yesterday that both of them lie dead on the fields of France. I have only you left and you are in Canada. Mother will not say for you to come back to France, but Mother will say, if you do not come now, do not ever come."

A nation will not die so long as her mothers have that spirit. Ah, when we cease to bleed we cease to bless. "I will buy it all at a full price. I will not offer that which costs me nothing — that which is easy. I will offer that which is stained by suffering, marked by blood. I will offer that." When our offering is like that we may be assured that it is acceptable unto God and that it will help to turn back from the gates of civilization the enemies of truth and righteousness and brotherhood.

I have not a shadow of a doubt about the final victory of Christ's cause. I have not a shadow of a doubt that He who died on that cross was the Son of God, that He was more than a mere man. Neither have I the shadow of a doubt that He who made the sacrifice on Calvary for human sin will ultimately have sway "from the river to the ends of the earth." That sacrifice of His Son is God's best. God can do no more. He has done His best in yonder sacrifice on Calvary's hill. Even so, when we poor creatures of time, creatures of a day compared with God, come with our talents, maybe just one, and say: "This offering represents all the industry and all the sacrifice and all the development and all the loyalty that I can put into it," we shall become more than conquerors through Jesus Christ, our Lord. It never fails.

When Weston, a brilliant young man, went down into Mexico as a missionary, quickly they took his life and threw his body out in the broiling sun, his eyes to be plucked out by the fowls of the air. When the word came back that he had been killed and his body thrown among the cactus bushes and his eyes plucked out by the fowls of the air, then forty young men said: "Send us to take his place." He had not died in vain.

When little Susie Parker went out to China, in the village they gave her a goodby service and the old father — the mother was dead — the old father was asked if he had something to say. The old man went to the platform and with his arm about Susie said: "I am not a speaker. I cannot talk but all I will say is that nothing I have is too good for my Jesus." Then Susie boarded the ship and before she reached the farther shore, the ship was sunk and the little girl was drowned in the ocean's depths.

The word came back and the people gathered in the same little church for a memorial service, and when the minister finished the service he said: "Is there anybody who has anything to say?" Susie's father stood up and said: "All I can say is what I said when she went away — 'nothing I have is too good for my Jesus.'" From that service thirty young women said: "We will go and take Susie's place." She had died for humanity and her service was not in vain.

When will we stop all our dodging and dreaming and self-deceiving? When will we learn to come with all our brains and hands and hearts and say: "Lord Jesus, one thing is of supreme concern and that is to give our all to make Thy will regnant throughout all the earth"? Thus, and thus only, as we give sacrificially self and service and substance, can we hope to attain unto the highest which God has designed for us.

> Carve thy name high over the shifting sand,
>   Where the steadfast rocks defy decay —
> All you can hold in your cold, dead hand
>   Is what you have given away.
>
> Build your pyramid skyward and stand,
>   Gazed at by millions, cultured they say —
> All you can hold in your cold, dead hand
>   Is what you have given away.
>
> Count your wide conquests of sea and land,
>   Heap up the gold, and hoard as you may —
> All you can hold in your cold, dead hand
>   Is what you have given away.
>
> Culture and fame and gold — ah so grand —
>   Kings of the salon, the mart, a day —
> All you can hold in your cold, dead hand
>   Is what you have given away.

Oh, men and women, my brothers and sisters, traveling with me fast to the realities of eternity, facing issues that are more important than life itself, let us dedicate our lives to Christ and let us do it now, the best we know how, while we pray.

CHAPTER III

The Still Small Voice

CHAPTER III

The Still Small Voice

~~~~~~

> *What doest thou here, Elijah?*
> —I KINGS 19:9

OUR text for this morning, a sharp question to the prophet Elijah when he was at one of the lowest ebbs of all his life, "What doest thou here, Elijah?" is found in the nineteenth chapter of the book of First Kings, the ninth verse.

You will agree that the prophet Elijah was one of the most inspiring personalities in all the unfolding stories of human life in the Scriptures or out of them, and that he was a good illustration of the truth of that old saying, "The best of men are but men at the best."

In Elijah we see the amazing changes that quickly take place in a person. Yesterday, on the heights of Carmel, one lone man stood against a field full of false prophets, courageously confronted them all and routed them completely; one man against hundreds. His behavior was so inspiring on the heights of Carmel that we are tempted to indulge in hero-worship. He seems almost more than human, but a few hours after that great experience a threatening message from the king's wife, Jezebel, told him that with another day, he would be where he had put those prophets of Baal.

Suddenly the majestic prophet of Mt. Carmel became a frightened and fleeing coward. With his servant he fled southward for 115 miles to Beersheba, where he left his servant. Then on for another day's journey he fled into the wilderness where he hid himself, utterly exhausted, under a juniper tree, and prayed to God that he might die. In other words, a great prophet of God quickly fell from the heights of triumph to the depths of despair.

But God knew and understood what had happened to his prophet. He knew that it was a physical rather than a moral or spiritual collapse. Therefore he sent an angel to minister unto the physical needs of Elijah. At that time Elijah needed food and drink and sleep more than anything else. When he had been refreshed by these, he resumed his flight and went 200 miles farther south to Horeb, near Mt. Sinai, where the Ten Commandments were given to Moses. There he hid in a cave. From the heights of Carmel to the cave of Horeb was a distance of more than 300 miles.

When a prophet of God has fetched fire from heaven, has taken the law into his own hands and has with a sword slain four hundred and fifty false prophets, has prayed down a flood to break a three-year drouth, and then on foot for twenty miles has outrun a king's chariot, he is a fit subject to be almost scared to death by the threat of a wicked woman. Jezebel really gave Elijah a frightful scare.

Many other men of God have had reactions somewhat similar to that of Elijah. One thinks of David saying: "The Lord is my light and my salvation; whom shall I fear? The Lord is the strength of my life; of whom shall I be afraid?" And yet, that same man can be heard saying on another occasion, when he was in a spell of despondency: "I shall one day perish at the hand of Saul."

One thinks of Simon Peter, the brave spokesman on the day of Pentecost, under whose sermon thousands were converted in one day. That same man on another occasion, even after Jesus had warned him, after all his promises and protestations of love and loyalty to Jesus, turned out to be a liar and added to his falsehood blasphemy and profanity, as he declared he knew not Jesus. All people, perhaps, at one time or another fail and fall into despondency and discouragement, and that is perhaps especially true of highly sensitive people.

42

The forms of discouragement are varied and many. They take one direction with one life, and another direction with another; but all people perhaps, at one time or another, feel the down-dragging power of despondency and discouragement.

If you read carefully into the life of William Shakespeare, you will find how he was fairly overwhelmed at times with depression and discouragement. So was it with Raphael, and even with great Spurgeon, the most wonderful gospel preacher of modern times. His friends have told me that at times the reactions which came to him were nothing short of pitiful. They would get around him and brace him and fortify him and tell him of someone who had been converted, and out of the depths he would climb and be once more on his feet.

At times I have seen Texas' great preacher, Dr. B. H. Carroll, in the very depths of depression and despondency. I saw him once when he was fairly overwhelmed by a period of depression and despondency which lasted for some time. An older man, one of his laymen, long trusted and loved by the preacher, in turn loved the preacher more than he loved any other man in the world. I heard that layman so inspirit and undergird, so cheer and encourage that great preacher that he quickly came out of the depth of despair and was on the hilltop again.

Now, we need to remember that the effects of depression, of despondency, of discouragement, are hurtful. That condition of mind is not Christian and it is displeasing to God. It is hurtful to ourselves and hurtful to others. We should set ourselves against the spirit of depression or despondency or discouragement, no matter what conditions may arise to distress us.

Let us look here again at this great man Elijah, who traveled the road of discouragement. First of all, let us look at his plight. He was in a serious condition as we see him in this chapter. In the language of the street, this big man was "down and out." He ran from a great victory, the greatest victory of all his life; ran clear away because of the threat of a wicked woman who told him: "By tomorrow, you shall be as these men you have destroyed: you shall be where they are." He ran for his life into the wilderness, and was under a juniper tree with his face to the ground, wailing out his prayer for God to let him die. There he lay.

He had become cynical. You know that the word "cynical" has an ugly meaning. It means "dog-like." A cynic snarls and bites and snaps, dog-like. The words "cynic" and "dog" go down to the same foundation root. Somebody gave a definition of a cynic a while ago. I think I have seen none better, namely: "A cynic is one who knows the price of everything but knows the value of nothing." I think that is a good definition of a cynic. And everybody is to set himself resolutely against cynicism.

Jesus said: "Judge not that ye be not judged, for with what judgment ye judge, ye shall be judged, and with what measure ye mete, it shall be measured unto you again." The Psalmist said: "Blessed is the man that walketh not in the counsel of the ungodly, nor standeth in the way of sinners, nor sitteth in the seat of the scornful." Let a man walk in the way of the ungodly, in their counsel, and stand in the presence of the God-despising, and the next time you hear of him, he will be far down the stream, sadly adrift.

I have known fine young men who started out with glorious promise, and high devotion to Christ, and I have seen them become so engrossed in their work that they forgot their church attendance. Bible reading and earnest, humble, daily, secret prayer were given up, and presently their heads were tossed high about this matter of Christianity and the church and the kingdom of God, about which they knew very little.

Now, Elijah was deeply depressed and discouraged. Yonder on the heights of Carmel, when he had routed those false prophets, he thought the victory was complete. He thought that he had gained the mastery over Ahab, the king, and Jezebel, the queen, but he had not. Evil does not readily abdicate or quit. You may rout it at one point, but it will show up at the next.

Elijah thought the battle was all over, but the battle had just begun. If we are to get the right conception of life, we must realize that the whole of life down here is a battle. We may have brief periods of peace, but they will not be for long. We have loads to carry, wars to wage. Jesus said: "In the world ye shall have tribulation: but be of good cheer; I have overcome the world." The final outcome will be victory, but you will have toiling; you will have trials after the most painful fashion. We are not to get any false notions that we are going out of one season of gracious delight into another, for when we get out of one season of delight, there will be a war and the world will be swimming in blood. This life is not a resting place for us. We are here with big loads to carry and big tasks to face and big duties to perform.

When the priests of Baal were defeated, Elijah fancied he was master of the situation. But he was mistaken. He had just started. He had all the evil forces against him. His faith suffered a temporary eclipse. He took his eyes away from God. On the heights of Carmel, when those men had failed in their fury and frenzy, Elijah had bowed before God and said: "Vindicate thy name, thy glory, thy being. Let these wicked men and all the world see that the Lord lives and reigns." He bowed like a little child in his prayer and God heard him and honored him and accepted his offering.

Under the juniper tree he wailed out his woes. His eyes were away from God. If any man takes his eyes away from God, he will be in darkness. If Christian people take their eyes away from God in this troubled, bludgeoned, unspeakable world situation through which we are passing, they, too, will be in utter darkness. If we take our eyes away from God, we shall be in trouble too terrible for man or angel to describe.

Simon Peter asked: "Let me walk to you on the water; let me come to you." And the Lord said: "Come!" And he started walking on the water, "but when he saw the boisterous wind, he was afraid and, beginning to sink, he cried saying: 'Lord save me.'" We shall go down in defeat if we take our eyes away from God. "Standeth God within the shadows, keeping watch above His own." Whatever comes, whatever goes, however dark the night, even Egyptian darkness, we are to keep our eyes on God. Job kept his eyes on God in midnight darkness, and the vindication that came for him was glorious beyond words.

Elijah had an exaggerated sense of his own importance. That is easy for a man to have in an hour of victory. At the cave in Horeb which was forty days journey from the juniper tree, God said: "What doest thou here, Elijah?" Then it was that the man who recently had utterly routed hundreds of false prophets before a great multitude of people, replied: "Well, I have been very jealous for God. I thought I could save Israel by slaying the false prophets and that Ahab and Jezebel would be utterly discredited. I thought we had them subdued and conquered, and lo, they seek my life, to take it away. I am the only man you have left. I am not better than my fathers were." Who said he was any better? He was not any better. Maybe not half as good. Maybe many of us are not half as good as our fathers and mothers were. Let us not get any exaggerated ideas of our own importance.

Somebody has defined discouragement in these words: "Discouragement is disenchanted egotism." That is a good definition. Disenchanted egotism! How terrible is egotism; for a man to imagine himself some great somebody, when apart from God he is nothing. Elijah had gone to Mt. Carmel, thinking that he was the only loyal friend God had

46

left in Israel. So far as he knew he had fought and won that great battle against Ahab and Jezebel and the priests of Baal all by himself with God's help. But ere the day was done his nerves gave way. A terrible reaction set in. The hero of Carmel became a frightened and fleeing coward.

We have already seen how the Lord treated Elijah, praying under the juniper tree that he might die. The first thing God did was to put him in good physical condition. Oh how wonderful are the ways of God! God sent his angel to minister unto him. He gave him something to eat, and allowed him to rest. He put him in good physical condition. Our bodies have great influence over us. There are many people moping in spirit and soul because their bodies are out of order. For that reason, when Jesus was here, right in the midst of a great campaign he had his disciples leave all their work and said unto them: "Come ye apart into a desert place and rest awhile." These bodies of ours are delicately constructed; they are to be undergirded, fortified, cared for; they are not to be abused or neglected or driven beyond their strength.

At Horeb God gave Elijah comfort by saying: "I have reserves in Israel. You are not the only one I have left. You are mistaken. I have seven thousand in Ahab's realm who have never bowed the knee to Baal." My own personal opinion is that these seven thousand men should not have been hiding out. They should have made themselves known to Elijah. When Elijah was fighting against those false prophets who sought to obliterate all that was good from the earth, I think they ought to have appeared and said: "Elijah, we will die with you. We are for you. We will fight with you. If it is dying, we will die with you." Men ought to link their lives with one another like that. But they did not appear, those seven thousand who had never bowed a knee to Baal.

Oh, what a comfort is the thought of God's reserves! I have found them in Hungary, that little land which has

47

been so wretchedly overrun. A thousand of our Baptist people there said to me: "In the years when you have been president of our world organization, we have prayed for you every day, by resolution passed in our convention; we have prayed for you every day that you will be a sane man and an inspiring helper such as we need in a time like this." And when in Rumania, I found sixteen hundred of our Baptist churches, some large and some small, people tossed and driven, persecuted, lashed, sent to concentration camps, kicked and cuffed about, but holding bravely on to Christ, unfearing, unhesitating, true. Out of the hills, out of the plains, out of the cities, and out of the country they come — God's brave men and women, ready to face whatever God may ask, that His cause may be cared for, and His name glorified — God's reserves!

At Horeb God gave Elijah a revelation of his compassion. There passed before Elijah a great wind, but the Lord was not in the wind. And there passed before him a great earthquake, but the Lord was not in the earthquake. And there passed before him a great fire, but the Lord was not in the fire. Then there came to Elijah, hiding there in a cleft in the rocks, a "still small voice," and Elijah knew that it was God's voice. Oh, how we are often swept away by the noisy, spectacular, barn-storming ways that mark the affairs of men. Elijah found out afresh the great compassion of God. There, alone, God said to him in that quiet voice, "What doest thou here, Elijah? You are out of your element; you are out of your territory; you are not at your post of duty. You have played the coward; you have run away, after the greatest victory of all your life. What doest thou here?"

Oh, my soul! How God comes to us also with the still small voice! In the quiet night when we cannot sleep, when we are isolated and detached from everybody else, when our souls are bared before God; if we listen we shall hear Him say: "What are you doing here? Is this the correct life for you to be living? Is this the right road for you to be traveling?"

Then the Lord said to Elijah: "I have work for you to do. Go anoint Jehu to be king over Israel, and anoint Elisha to be your successor in the prophetic office. You will find him in his field plowing. Go and anoint him. Go to work!"

Now, in that same way the Lord marks the way for us, the way of victorious behavior. Many a man is consumed with doubt. He is pierced through and through in his soul with questions, with spiritual doubt, because of his idleness. Get to work! Go to your classes, your family, your church, your business. Get to your work with all possible diligence and devotion. Go about it with unselfishness. That is the way to victory.

I think that was a wonderful scene when Lord North, the commander of the British forces, got back to England, having evacuated a vast number of those men caught in a trap up there in Flanders. I think his words, when felicitations were showered upon him because of his safe return, will do for us today. He said: "Oh, that is not the important thing, not for me to be back in safety, but for my army, my men. It matters little about one man. It matters much about these men. It is these men you are to glory in, and to thank God for," said the British commander. The right view of life is to live for others.

I have travelled over much of Holland. Happy Holland, home-loving Holland, great-hearted people of Holland! I have been there several times. They told me a story about Princess Wilhelmina, their queen until recently. They said that when she came to the throne, as a young girl, she was with her mother on the balcony, and below them were the cheering thousands. She turned to her mother and said: "Do all these people belong to me?" And the mother said: "No, dear, you belong to all these people!" That is the true way of life. You belong to all these people. Oh, preacher, you belong to the people! Teacher, you belong to the people! Man or woman, whatever your talent or calling, you belong to humanity. "What doest thou here, Elijah?"

Oh, man or woman, are you at the place you ought to be? Are you doing your duty full length and full strength? Oh, men and women, are you being true to God? If you are neglecting your duty anywhere, stir out of your lethargy and be done with neglect. What are you doing for God and humanity, oh soul, hurrying through time into eternity? Are you living the life God asked you to live, which, if not lived, will mark your life for failure and self-destruction?

Are you here today saying: "I have not begun to live yet, because up until today I have thrust God away, but no more will I close the door of my heart to Him; today and now I make my surrender to Him"?

Who says, "I want to link my life openly with Christ, and with his church and his people"? Come boy or girl, man or woman, father or mother, or stranger within our gates today! Who says: "Today God has spoken to me; I am not where I ought to be; I am not doing what I ought to do, but I turn about with God's help and I will follow Christ; I trust Him; I surrender to Him and from today I follow Christ"?

Then come! Come as we sing: "I am Thine, O Lord, I have heard Thy voice."

CHAPTER IV

Elisha's Call to Service

CHAPTER IV

Elisha's Call to Service

~~~~~~

> *So he departed thence, and found
> Elisha the son of Shaphat, who was
> plowing with twelve yoke of oxen be-
> fore him, and he with the twelfth: and
> Elijah passed by him, and cast his
> mantle upon him.*
> —I KINGS 19:19

THE desire and the effort to perpetuate that which is good in other lives that are to come after us is one of the highest and worthiest of desires and efforts possible to a human life.

Elijah lived in a time when corruption in the country had reached frightful proportions, and the vices of the people threatened their destruction. He cried aloud and spared not. He rebuked with all faithfulness, and yet he became discouraged. One of the most discouraged men the world ever saw was Elijah after his memorable contest with the priests of Baal on Mount Carmel. So discouraged was he that he became petulant and begged for the privilege of dying. God, in His gracious way, refreshed and revived him, and then said to him, "Look about for some man to help you. Look about for some successor."

And from that retreat where, a little while ago Elijah lay upon his face crying his heart out because of discouragement, Elijah arose and went by the way of the wilderness toward Damascus and found Elisha, plowing in the field. Passing by him, Elijah threw his mantle upon Elisha. He meant to indicate by that: "You, O Elisha, are to be linked with me in my responsible work. You are to carry it on when I have gone. My mission is to be transmitted to you and become your mission." That was the meaning of casting his mantle upon Elisha.

I have no faith in the religion of that man who has no interest in posterity. I would not risk his chance at the bar of God. One of the strongest evidences that one is God's child is his deep concern about the kingdom of God after he shall have passed away. Elijah gave full evidence that he was a child of God when he manifested deep concern as to who would be his successor in his prophetic ministry.

That expression, "casting his mantle upon him," is so striking it has become proverbial. When a great man dies we think, "Who will take his place?" That is one of the first thoughts we have when a good and noble man passes away. Oh, the sense of bereavement, of poverty, of need that grips our hearts when good men fall at their posts, and some one must take up their work. It has become proverbial, this matter of the mantle descending from one life to another.

In a group of men last week I could hear them discussing, though I took no part in the discussion, who could take the place of this man and that man in this city. The time of their departure will not be forever prolonged, and when they go, who will stand in their shoes and take up their work? I confess to a feeling of deep seriousness, when I heard those men discuss that matter.

What man does not remember when the old preachers used to stand up and pour out their hearts on the question of who should succeed them in the ministry? When I was a lad I heard those men who had given their lives to the work so talk about their mantle descending upon others that I was deeply impressed by them as I heard them press that great matter. Perhaps that had much to do with my entering the ministry in the after years.

Who will take our place, who will perpetuate the good in our lives? What more meaningful question could we lay to heart than that? One of the most noble ends has been gained by a useful life if that life can inspire others to take up the work and carry on.

You will notice in this incident, so significant, that God calls busy men. There is no record of His calling an idler. Idlers are not promoted in the kingdom of God. Elisha was tilling the soil and following the plow, a man engaged in honest work. Upon him God laid the prophetic mantle. When Jesus called the Apostles, He chose busy men. The busiest men in the world are those whom God often calls to large responsibilities. Idlers do not make good servants of God.

The response of Elisha to Elijah's call was something glorious. Elisha immediately left his plowing, said goodbye to his loved ones, made his sacrifice complete, burned every bridge behind him, and became a great and worthy successor to Elijah.

Passing by the details of this incident, let us come to the one great point, the practical lesson. What is it? The incident points out for us the unspeakable blessedness of worthily perpetuating in another the good influence of one's own life. That is the practical significance of this old-time incident. See what this meant to Elisha himself. It awakened him; it inspired him; it set him forth on a career of enlarged usefulness for the world's good and for God's glory. That was the meaning for Elisha, and from that hour the Scriptures picture these two men as they went on together, Elijah telling the young man his hopes and plans. The Scripture says that Elisha arose and followed after Elijah and ministered unto him.

Oh, how much Elisha meant to Elijah and how much in turn Elijah meant to Elisha! It was like the love that existed between Paul and Timothy. Paul's great desire was that the preaching of God's word should go on in Asia, and elsewhere. Diligently, he sought to train Timothy. He searched him and filled him with great ideals that he might have com-

55

pelling visions. Think how much Timothy meant to Paul and how much Paul meant to Timothy.

Some one came to John Knox, who was naturally a timid and shrinking young man, and said, "The condition of Scotland is such, Knox, that some one must take hold of it. God is dishonored. Religion is formal and perfunctory. Knox, you have latent power, tremendous power. You are the man to remedy this." How can we measure the value of that conversation with Knox, who by it was sent out on his immortal career! Scotland is his monument forever!

Who knows the latent possibilities in one human life, even an unpromising life? Sometimes the most unpromising lads came out of their seeming mediocrity with a sweep of power that astonishes all. Who knows the slumbering-powers in any life about us when charged with great purposes and fired with high ideals for the good of man and for the glory of God? Elijah did all that for Elisha.

Sir Henry Drummond said, "I have made many discoveries, but my greatest discovery was the discovery of Michael Faraday." To wake up a life, to imbue it with great hopes and high purposes, that is life's greatest accomplishment. Elijah did that for Elisha, and since that time men by the countless thousands have done the same thing. Here in this city are men who came to positions of great worth and great importance in the affairs of state and church, in the world of society and business, in all professions of life; men and women touched by some life when that life's mantle descended; men who felt the burning fire of a life worthy and noble, and were influenced thereby. The mantle had descended and the city was richer and brighter in every way because of their lives. Oh, to wake up a life, to change it, to shame it out of sordid ideals and low visions! What can compare with that in all the purposes and privileges of human life? It behooves us to be ever on the alert to speak a word in season that will galvanize a soul into vital action.

See what this incident meant to the world. Not only was Elisha aroused but there was the launching of an influence so great and gracious that it largely changed Israel for good. To be sure these two men were very different. Elijah was an agitator; Elisha a reformer. Elijah slew with the sword; Elisha came pouring oil on the troubled waters. But the work of each was inspired by God and divinely directed.

Elijah lived in a time when the axe had to be laid at the roots of the tree, when great evils had to be smitten hip and thigh. Each man had diverse gifts, and there comes in the glory of individuality. Men are not made on the same mold. Destroy individuality and you destroy a man's possibilities. Men are not made just alike. God desires your individuality, your own self, not another, to be used in a certain way. Let nothing destroy your individuality. You will come to your highest and your best by the development of your own individuality.

Elijah had his work and did it in his own peculiar way, and Elisha came and did his work differently, but effectively. One sows and another reaps. One life joins to another. David could not build the temple, but it was left to his son, Solomon, to build the magnificent structure which he planned.

Oh, what it means to the world worthily and well to impart noble desires and inspirations to other lives. The lessons of this old-time incident are for you and for me. They are as fresh and practical for us today as they were in the days of Elijah and Elisha.

Here is a profound message for those who are parents. They are to live worthily through their children. This is their greatest earthly responsibility. If parents care not for the lives of their children in the noblest, the most unselfish way, they are not worthy to be parents. This message is one of tremendous moment. The supreme task of every parent is to seek worthily to perpetuate the best in the children given them of God. That is the supreme task of parents and

57

they cannot avoid that responsibility. If children are neglected and influenced evilly, it is an unending tragedy. A disaster has been done that will be felt through the ages if parents do not by precept and example strive to transmit to their children the highest ideals and noblest virtues of their own lives.

The father is the priest of the house and the head of the home, just as God appointed him. Nor can man abdicate his position for business reasons, nor can he plead that he can not give time enough, nor can he seek to transfer the responsibility to the mother or to the church or to society. The father has done a disastrous thing if he forgets that for his child he is the priest, and the child should be able to believe in the father's religion with all his being. In this day of rush and drive much needs to be said to the father regarding his responsibility, that responsibility which nobody else can assume.

And how important the mother's place, how great her responsibility in the family! The first teacher is the mother, and her position is simply incomparable. "France," said the great Napoleon, "needs more than all else, good mothers." And the same may be said of every land in every time.

We do not need screaming reformers, as much as they may be needed, as we need good mothers, who seek to pour holy and heavenly words into the ears of their children, whispering words so chaste, so unselfish, so good that their power can never be broken. Mother, God has given you children! To these children you owe your best thought and guidance. Mother, put your best into the thoughts and minds of your children. Great is their need. Exhibit before them the joyful life, the patient life, the life laid on the altar, the life that does not complain, the life that is not selfish.

Do you know what great men thought of their mothers? Benjamin West, when he was great in the world's eye as an artist, with deep emotion said, "When I was a little boy, I looked at my baby sister and drew a rough sketch of her, and when Mother saw it, she cried and hugged me and then kissed me, and that kiss made me the artist I am!" Oh, the place of a mother nobody can take! And there is no life comparable to hers in the transmission of the best through her children. A great lesson for parents comes out of this old-time incident of Elijah's mantle being cast upon Elisha.

Attend to the great matter of ordering your house in righteousness and godliness. The home is the first great divine institution, established in Eden. It was here before the state, before the church. Before sin came to defile the world and the darkness of death to sadden, God gave us the home. It is at the base of every great and good and noble thing in the world. Let the godliness and the holiness of the family be destroyed and you hit at the very vitals of all life that is worth while. The pulpit is insipid and power-less if it be not buttressed with homes of godliness. The lesson is clear and powerful that the homes be ordered in righteousness! There is no grander sight on this earth than the well-ordered Christian home!

This old-time message is a message for teachers also. How gracious and wonderful are the privileges of the teacher! The teacher in a marvelous way may fashion and mold the lives of his pupils, and like Elijah may put the mantle of a glorious life on his pupil. What a lesson for a teacher!

The teacher who does not tremble daily before his great task, his mighty responsibility, is not worthy to teach half a minute. Trevonius, the teacher of Martin Luther, said that he never came before a class of boys without taking off his hat to those noble boys. When asked why he did that he said, "I do not know but that I am lifting my hat to a man who shall shake the world." Martin Luther went out and made every throne in the world to totter and brought a new day mentally and morally to the world.

Frederick of Prussia was having a great fete, and as he marched at the head of his troops there was an old, white-haired man in the crowd who, beside himself with joy, cried again and again at the top of his voice, "I taught him. I taught him!" And all over this land are teachers who can look on great legislators and their joyful shout can be "I taught him! I taught him!" Can the teacher think of his great task save with a fast beating heart? Garfield's teacher had much to do with making him President, and Garfield acknowledged that fact in a beautiful tribute.

Two things there are that make the teacher's task unspeakably serious. The first is his responsibility. Oh, how the teacher will impart his teaching unconsciously! His greatest influence is an unconscious influence. We impart ourselves. If you are bad yourself, the bad will be imparted; and if you are high minded and noble, these characteristics will be imparted. I do not remember word by word half a dozen sentences that were taught me by all my teachers, but I remember those men. I remember their shame when a boy did wrong; their praise when a boy did right. Oh the responsibility of a teacher!

The second thing that makes the teacher's task a serious one is his authority. What a position to occupy! What a mission he is sent to perform! How it ought to sober any man or woman when responsibility and authority are understood as they ought to be. If you were studying Jesus Christ of Nazareth as a teacher, just from the viewpoint of authority, you would get a better lesson on pedagogics than from any book on pedagogy in all the world. No teacher ever taught as did Jesus of Nazareth. If your life is narrow and selfish, you will put that spirit into the life and brain of every child you teach. What a message for teachers and for others as well.

There is the doctor! What a calling is his! What a sacred service is that in which he labors, and how the best in him may be perpetuated if he be willing to have it so! What an opportunity is his to benefit mankind and glorify God!

And the lawyers! The great, high-minded lawyer; what a task is his in the affairs of earth, and what an opportunity to gladden mankind and glorify God has the worthy lawyer! I mean the high-minded lawyer who, under no circumstance, would do any dishonorable thing.

Then the philanthropist! One of them said to me not long ago, "I have not one concern for the years to come, whether they be many or few, but to make my means count the most for the Master. I have entered into a compact with God that if He will let my business prosper I will leave my money for that specific work of His, for which I live." Oh, the noble philanthropist! He will start a thousand streams in the desert of life, and long after he shall have passed away his work for the welfare of his fellowman will remain.

Oh, the simple lesson in this incident! Let us live so that our lives may live on! Do you know the meaning of the term "Son of Perdition" applied to Judas Iscariot? Rightly translated, it is a "child of waste." Oh, the waste of a life that does not conform to God's plan! Was there ever tragedy comparable to that? It will not be your tragedy if your life is anchored on Jesus Christ. That life which is not so anchored fails of the great purpose of God concerning it.

What God requires of us is that we give our best to Him and to our own generation. Do that and we may know that what has been good and true and Christ-like in our lives will be passed on to bless succeeding generations. The good is more enduring than the evil. We are told in the Ten Commandments that the iniquity of the fathers is visited upon the children unto the third and fourth generation of them that hate God; but that God's mercy will be extended unto a thousand generations of them that love God and keep his commandments. My earnest and oft-repeated prayer is that the present members of this great church may live so worthily and righteously that their godly influence, like a heaven-sent mantle may rest upon the lives of future generations of those who become members of this household of God. My beloved people, yours is a vast and God-given responsibility and opportunity. Shirk not the responsibility, and make the most of the opportunity. With Christ's help you can influence thousands for good in the generations to come.

CHAPTER V

The Bible Lost and Found

C H A P T E R   V

The Bible Lost and Found

~~~~~~

> *And Hilkiah the high priest said unto*
> *Shaphan the scribe, I have found the*
> *book of the law.*
>
> —II KINGS 22:8

THIS morning I speak to you on the subject: The Bible, Lost and Found. The text I have chosen carries us back to the days of the Old Testament kings, and at this particular time Josiah was the king, one of the best of all the kings of Judah. His reign began at the early age of eight. The Bible tells us that at the age of sixteen he began to seek after God, and at the age of eighteen young Josiah began a national reformation following the finding and reading of the long-lost Book of the Law.

A positive part of Josiah's campaign was the restoration of Solomon's great temple at Jerusalem. The temple and its services of worship had been sadly neglected for many years. It is unthinkable that the nation would have allowed that glorious structure to be filled with rubbish and left in shameful disrepair. But such was the case and we now know why it was. Workmen of all kinds were employed for that vast cleansing and renovating task. In the midst of the cleaning out of the rubbish Hilkiah, the high priest, found a dust-covered scroll which was called the Book of the Law — the laws of God given through Moses. In other words, Hilkiah found the lost Bible of that time.

For a long time the rulers, the priests and the masses of the people of Judah had been ignorant of their Bible which was called the Book of the Law. That fact accounts for the spread of Baal worship through Judah, and it also explains the neglect of the temple and its services of worship of Jehovah. It likewise explains why the nation had sunk to such a low moral and spiritual condition.

When Hilkiah, the high priest, came across the long lost scroll and saw that it was the law of God as given by Moses, he brought it to Shaphan, the scribe. Then Shaphan took the book at once to King Josiah and said, "Hilkiah, the high priest, rummaging in the temple, came across this book."

"Read it to me," commanded the king, and Shaphan began to read. Presently Josiah, the king, was in utter consternation as he realized that the nation had utterly departed from the counsel of God. Then young Josiah humbled himself in the dust. "The reformation," Josiah said, "shall begin with the king. The head of this nation will put himself in the dust and repent in sackcloth and ashes." And then to all his officers and to those close to him he said, "We must repent for our derelictions, for all our neglect, for all our sins, or the nation will be destroyed." Thus throughout all Judah there began a reformation; the king was spared and his people were spared. The lost Bible had been found.

Josiah assembled leaders of the people from all over the nation and in solemn assembly read to them the long lost Book of the Law. Their reaction was like that of the king. They were astonished; they were humiliated; and they were penitent when they realized how far the nation had departed from the laws of God. They agreed with their young king that heroic measures of reform should be adopted at once. They favored the full restoration of the temple and its worship of almighty God. Not only that, but they decided to back Josiah in his drastic campaign of wiping out every vestige of Baal worship in the land and also numerous other forms of idolatry which, like cancers, had eaten into the vitals of the nation. All of this was brought about by the re-discovery of God's inspired Word.

That ancient incident holds lessons of solemn warning and of hearty encouragement for us. It shows us the tragic ills which beset any people who lose sight of God's Word and neglect His worship. But it also shows us the blessed results when people give God's Word and will and worship their rightful place in their lives.

The sad truth is that people may lose the Bible today even as it was lost in the time of Josiah. The Bible may be lost today by *neglect*. We can go our ways, looking after our businesses, looking after our tasks, looking after the concerns and calls of our daily lives and may lose this book of the law of God. The Bible may be lost by neglect. There it lies on the parlor table; there it rests on the mantel, and yet weeks go by, it may be, and even months, and this book of the law of God is not consulted. With all its counsel, all its wisdom, all its light and leading, it is not consulted at all. As we go our busy ways here and there, the Bible, God's law, the lamp for our feet may be lost by neglect.

How else may it be lost? It may be lost by *substitution*. That is to say, we may put other things in its place. Jesus said to the scribes and Pharisees of His day: "Ye have made the commandments of God of no effect by your traditions." These scribes and Pharisees, who were teachers of religion, set aside the Bible, the law of God, the divine revelation to men; set it aside by human commandments, human traditions. If we put anything in the place of the Bible, then the Bible is lost thereby. One of the tragedies of the world this fair morning is the reading, both good and bad, which is substituted for this book of the centuries.

It is possible to lose the Bible ourselves by substituting a great deal of good reading for it. One of the perils to the preacher today is that he will go there to his shelf and read what the scholars, critical and practical, say about the Bible, without coming to the Bible for himself and letting the Bible speak to him, and letting God through the Bible say to him what God wants the Bible to say to him. We can

67

lose the Bible by substituting lesson helps and quarterlies and commentaries, and books on devotional reading.

Time and again I am asked by people that grope, beaten down by the flail of disappointment and bereavement and suffering: "Tell me some good devotional book to read, to help me as I grope in the darkness." Why, the devotional books of this world are like little candles lighted by men compared with the sun, when we bring these books alongside the holy Word of God. The fourteenth chapter of John, and the twenty-third Psalm, and the eighth chapter of Romans have more in them of comfort and reinforcement and inspiration and impulse upward than all the books of earth written by men — three chapters in the Bible. And so we are in danger of losing the Bible by substituting other things in its place.

Nor is that all. We are in danger of losing the Bible by *mutilation,* by taking out a little here, and a little there, and casting the other aside. You cannot treat the Bible like that. The Word of God which we have today has been tried through the long centuries. The searchlight of criticism, both from foes and friends, has been focused during the long years on this book of God. All the books put together have not suffered a thousandth part of the testing to which the Word of God has been subjected. We are in danger of losing the Bible when we cut out this and cut out that and change this and change that.

I have read every attack I can find on the Bible; and yet I tell you, as I come back and bring brain and conscience and life to the Word of God and examine the cavilings and the attacks brought against it, I believe it without wavering from the records in the Pentateuch to the last syllable in the last book of Revelation. The Word of God is a tested word. Do not mutilate it now by cutting it to pieces.

Nor is that all. We may lose the Word of God by *disobeying* it. Let a man have light and fail to use it, and his light will turn into darkness. There are many men today who have become skeptics because they had light and did not live up to it. If a man does not use his light, that light will turn into darkness. If a man has a conviction on any question and represses it, that conviction will get weaker every hour he lives. A man is to utter his belief. A man is to make known his conviction. Every time a man utters his conviction he is thenceforth stronger because of such utterance. Even so, if a man has light from the Word of God, and ignores it, and disregards it, Jesus Himself teaches that his light shall be turned into darkness. That man who had one talent and would not use it had that talent taken from him. A man who has light and will not use it has the light taken from him. A man who knows his duty and refuses to do it gets deeper into the darkness every hour.

When one has the will of God revealed to him in the Bible on any question, he is to follow that will of God. This holy Bible is the infallible rule of faith and practice. God has spoken to men by the Holy Spirit and men thus inspired have preserved His counsels for the world's weal, and here it is in a book for us, the infallible rule of faith and practice.

If the Bible be lost, what else will be lost? You could better afford to lose every book on the face of the earth this morning than to lose this Bible. The Bible has inspired earth's best literature, best art, best music, best laws, best religion, best social order, best civilization. The Bible is God's written revelation of Himself and of His plan of salvation. It tells men how to be saved, how to live with each other, how to go to Heaven. And best of all it tells us about Jesus Christ, our Saviour and Lord, our Substitute, our Sinbearer, our Redeemer, who purchased our salvation with His own precious blood, shed on Calvary's cruel cross that we might have eternal life.

Oh, can you imagine a world so tragically impoverished by the loss of the Bible that there would be no reason for the poet to write:

> *A glory gilds the sacred page,*
> *Majestic as the sun!*
> *It gives its light to every age;*
> *It gives, but borrows none.*

Or that there would be no occasion for a friend of God to sing:

> *Holy Bible, Book divine,*
> *Precious treasure, thou art mine.*

Shouts of praise and thanksgiving from our hearts should reach to the throne of God that we have the Holy Bible, every page of which is open to all who desire it. It has been printed in nearly all the languages of earth. Its circulation is one of the wonders of the modern world. It is still the miracle book of all the ages. Its light has power to dispel the darkness from the hearts of individuals, families, tribes, and nations.

You do not wonder that such a book as that is being urged upon our soldier boys everywhere. You do not wonder that the effort is being made to put that book in the hands of every soldier going forth to the camp and the field. And you are not surprised at the inscription which the President ordered put in every Bible given to the armed forces. Let me read it to you: "The Bible is the word of light. I beg that you will read it and find this out for yourselves. Read not little snatches here and there, but long passages that will really be the road to the heart of it. You will find it full not only of real men and women, but also of the things you have wondered about and been troubled about all your life, as men have been always, and the more you read the Bible the more it will become plain to you what things in this world are worth while and what are not; what things make men to be loyal, right dealing, speaking the truth, readiness to give everything for what they think their duty, and most of all the wish that they may have the real approval of the Christ who gave everything for them; and the things that are guaranteed to make men unhappy, selfishness, cowardice, greed, and everything that is low and mean. You will read all that in the Bible. When you have read the Bible you will know that it is the Word of God, because you will have found it the key to your own heart, your own happiness, and your own duty."

For all these reasons and many others, I urge that we come back to the Bible and read it, and know it and follow it, the Holy Word of God. Let it be an open Book, a used Book. Let this Book make its full impact on your minds, your hearts and your wills. Let it be a lamp unto your feet and a light unto your path.

Oh, men and women, especially those of you who are parents or teachers, let me, with every ounce of influence I may have, urge that you become so saturated with the teachings of this Book that your own lives will be divinely enriched by the wisdom, the grace and the power that come from God and, being thus enriched, may you do all in your power to give to your children and your pupils a knowledge of and a love for this greatest of all books. See to it that every one of them has his or her own Bible. Let it be lovingly inscribed as a gift from father or mother or teacher.

You parents can do no wiser thing than to have a set time for the reading of God's Word to the youngsters there in your home. Not only read it to them, but explain it to them as best you can. At other times tell to them some of the wonderful stories found in the Bible. Children and older people, too, love the Bible stories more than any others in all the world, and the children will remember them to old age.

Oh, parents and teachers, there is no estimating the eternal value of what you do to implant the Word of God in the minds and hearts of impressionable young people! Nothing you can do is more vital or more worthwhile in God's sight!

I told a group of you, on coming back from the West some weeks ago, of the conversion of a notorious character in the far West, a man who had killed several men. I do not know anything about the merits or demerits of the awful tragedies, but he was sent to prison for a long time. His own body was marred and scarred by bullets and one arm gone. He came to the meeting out of idle curiosity, a man nearly seventy years of age, and then he tarried and became interested, and by and by, after days of darkness, the poor fellow humbly made public confession of Christ as his Saviour. And when later I talked with him, he said to me, with his great frame quivering as though he were a tree riven by the lightning: "My mother died when I was about six years old, but before she died, my mother — and there was never better — taught me the Word of God. But I forgot all about it, for she died and I had no friend left. I have been a rover, a wanderer, a wretched sinner; but as I have heard you preach these three or four days, those sentences which mother taught me, which I had forgotten for fifty or sixty years, burned in my soul like a furnace, and while you preached I could see written in great characters those verses out of the Bible that mother taught me before I was six years of age."

The seed planted by that mother in the life of her child had lain dormant for fifty years. Then in his old age, when I preached the gospel within his hearing, the Holy Spirit took those gospel truths and let them become like rain and sunshine falling on the long dormant seed of the mother's sowing. That seed germinated and brought forth repentance and faith. That man was gloriously saved before that meeting ended.

Oh, the Bible has great appeal for children and for young people who become acquainted with it and for old people who learned to love it during their earlier years. But the Bible makes a powerful appeal to red-blooded men in the prime of life, because the Bible has so much of virility and wisdom and heroism and strength in it. Every busy man of affairs, engaged in the daily struggles and battles of life ought to read the Bible every day. He may run railroads, but he ought to read the Bible regularly. He may be mayor of a city or governor of a state or president of a nation, but he ought to read the Bible daily. He may be a great teacher, doctor or lawyer, but he ought to read the Bible every day. If the mighty business and professional men of this nation would read and study and know their Bibles the future of our beloved country would be blessedly assured.

Oh, my dear people, let us in every possible way magnify the Bible in every phase of our church life, in our home life, in our business and professional life, in every realm in which we touch the lives of others. Let us thank God continually for the Bible and do all within our power to cause this Book and its truths to have free course unto the ends of the earth. It is God's Word to a lost and needy world!

Let us pray.

CHAPTER VI

Mutilating God's Word

C H A P T E R   V I

Mutilating God's Word

~~~~~~

And it came to pass, that when Jehudi had read three or four leaves of that scroll, Jehoiakim cut it with the penknife, and cast it into the fire, until the entire scroll was consumed in the fire.

—JEREMIAH 36:23

THIS morning I spoke to you about one of the very best men in all the Bible, King Josiah of Judah. We saw how he behaved when his attention was brought face to face with the Word of God. We saw how that Word of God had been lost, that scroll on which God's law far back yonder was written, before printing came into vogue. That scroll was lost, and the nation groped in darkness and plunged downward in sin. When at last the scroll was found and read to the young king Josiah, he abased himself before God in the sight of all the people, and led his people in confession and penitence. His example influenced the whole nation and Judah was restored to a glorious place for a season in the sight of God. Josiah was one of the best kings and one of the best men in the Old Testament.

Now this evening we are to study about his successor, Jehoiakim, who was one of the worst men in all the Bible story. When he came to the throne of Judah and was reigning, the prophet Jeremiah at God's command uttered faithful warnings and counsels for the good of the king and the whole nation, summoning the king and the whole nation to right relations toward God. The news of Jeremiah's words reached the ears of king Jehoiakim, and the king sent a messenger for that scroll on which those words were written for the counsel of the king and the nation.

The scroll was brought into the presence of the king and read to him and his fawning courtiers. Now our text comes in:

> *And it came to pass, that when Jehudi had read three or four leaves of that scroll, Jehoiakim cut it with the penknife, and cast it into the fire, until the entire scroll was consumed in the fire.*

You see at once a marked difference between the behavior of Josiah and Jehoiakim. When God's law was read to Josiah from the scroll, he abased himself in penitence and led his nation in the right course. But when the scroll on which was written God's decrees concerning the nation was read to Jehoiakim, he refused to hear much of it. When the reader had read three or four leaves, the haughty, self-willed king snatched the roll from the reader, and with his penknife cut it into pieces and flung it into the fire where it was consumed.

Why did Jehoiakim do that? The primary reasons for his course were evidently two. For one thing, that law of God on that scroll was a message that the self-willed king did not desire to hear. He was pursuing a life of ease, of riotous self-indulgence, of exceeding wickedness, and that roll of God summoned men to face the truth that as men sow so shall they reap. Jehoiakim did not want to hear that. He wanted to go right on, undisturbed in his life of licentiousness and wickedness, and he did not want to hear any such warning, any such counsel.

A man's infidelity is often in his heart rather than in his head. I have dealt long enough with men's spiritual problems to find out that much of the infidelity in this world is lodged in the heart and not in the head at all. Full many a time, men do not want to hear God's law and do not want His counsel and His light to shine upon their pathway, because their deeds are evil. It was that way with Jehoiakim, the proud and evil young king of Judah.

And then in addition to his desire not to hear God's message at all was that other patent fact revealed clearly there in the story. The young man was swept on with egregious conceit of his own power. Power of any kind tends to make men proud, arrogant, haughty and self-willed. Many a king has failed even after years of splendid reign because power turned his head and corrupted his heart. Many a ruler who began most hopefully has fallen from the heights into the depths because pride came as the result of power. That was the case with Jehoiakim. He was haughty and self-willed because he had power. And so when the scroll of God's law was brought into the king's presence and read to him and he saw where it was leading, how pungent its counsels were, how serious was its indictment of every evil way, he flushed with anger and his anger deepened until presently he rudely snatched the roll out of the reader's hands and with his penknife cut it into shreds, and flung it into the fire where it was consumed. It is one of the most wretched pictures of any man in all Bible history.

Again, at God's command Jeremiah dictated, and again the scribe Baruch wrote, and the scroll was reproduced, giving counsel and light to the people. But Jehoiakim led the whole nation on the downward path and came to a tragic death. His epitaph was written later by this same prophet Jeremiah, who summed up the death and burial of Jehoiakim at last in these blunt words: "Jehoiakim was buried with the burial of an ass."

Jehoiakim sought to get rid of the word of God, to cut it to pieces, to burn it in the fire, to get it out of his way. Now, my friends, this incident raises a question for our meditation this evening. What if men could get rid of the Bible, cut it all to pieces with their knives, and then, all torn and dismantled from the cutting, fling it into the fire, there to be utterly consumed? What if men could get rid of the

Bible? What then? Suppose you could get rid of it, what then? What if men should take the Bible and fling it impiously into the fire, until every leaf of it is burned up right before them, what then?

Now there are several things for us to remember. If we should get rid of the Bible there are several great facts that would remain, Bible or no Bible. What are they? Though we should get rid of the Bible, the fact of *God* remains. The Bible does not make God. God made the Bible. The Bible reveals God. The Bible nowhere argues for the fact of God. The very first verse of the Bible begins with the assumption of God. "In the beginning God created the heavens and the earth." From the first verse to the last the Bible assumes that there is a God. The Bible tells us what kind of God He is. The Bible tells us what the will of God is toward us. The Bible tells what God wishes. We may burn the Bible. We may cut it into shreds. We may refuse to read it. We may be ignorant of it. And yet the Bible does not change the fact of God. God is, God exists, and God will continue, whatever we may do to the Bible.

The Bible is the lamp God puts into men's lives to show them how to live and how to die. The Bible is the great counsel book given by God that men may not grope in the darkness but may see the right path and travel in it. And so, though we may burn and destroy the Bible, though we may refuse to read the Bible and know what its precepts and counsels are, we cannot by such course get rid of God. God will remain, whatever we do with the Bible.

What else? Suppose we do get rid of the Bible, burn it, destroy it, what else is left? *Sin* is left. The Bible does not make sin. The Bible tells about sin. The Bible pictures sin. The Bible warns us against sin. And though we should burn the Bible and get rid of it and refuse to know what it says, yet sin would remain just the same to blind and deaden and destroy us.

Then there is the fact of *conscience*. God has put that monitor in every human breast, that monitor called conscience, that God-given faculty whereby we may discern between right and wrong. The faculty of conscience is left whatever we do with the Bible.

All history attests the awful power of conscience. Take the case of Nero, that bloody ruler who at last reached the culmination of his course of unspeakable cruelty and crimes by murdering his own mother. History tells us that Nero made his outcry night after night, saying: "I can hear the groans of my mother from her far off grave." It was his conscience at work. Take the case of King Richard on Bosworth Field. King Richard tells us that the ghost of all the victims he had murdered, including his own wife, paraded before his tent and made their outcry against his course. It was conscience making its outcry. Shakespeare has him to say:

> *My conscience hath a thousand several tongues,*
> *And every tongue brings in a several tale,*
> *And every tale condemns me for a villain.*

Take the case of that noted murderer some years ago, one of the leading teachers of the country, in one of the leading universities, Professor Webster. At last, through a trail of circumstantial evidence the guilt of murder was fastened upon the noted teacher, and he was condemned to death. He lay in his cell awaiting the day of execution and he offered his protest, saying: "The keepers of this prison and the prisoners day and night cry out to me, 'O you bloody man!' Wherever I go the keepers of the prison look at me and say, 'O you bloody man!'" Professor Webster offered his protest against any such cruelty, and they set a watchman there to ascertain whether or not these outcries he professed to hear were real or imaginary. They were found to be hallucinations. It was the awful outcry of conscience in his heart, the awful element within him saying that though a man may

81

fling the Bible and its light in the fire, conscience is still left to make its awful cry within the man.

We recall that Herod got rid of John the Baptist, silenced that great prophet tongue, took his head from his shoulders, and cast the body out as offal for the vultures and for the dogs. Months went by and Herod heard rumors of a strange personality out in the country whom everybody went out to hear, a man who spake as never man spake. Then Herod, all affrighted, rose up and blurted out his cry: "I suspect you are talking about John the Baptist, that man whom months ago I killed." That was Herod's conscience at work. You cannot get rid of conscience.

Byron went his way sowing to the flesh, but at the last he voiced his agony and loss in these oft-quoted lines:

> My days are in the yellow leaf;
> The flowers and fruits of love are gone;
> The worm, the canker, and the grief
> Are mine alone!

You must reckon with conscience. You may burn the Bible, as did Jehoiakim, but you will have God left, and you will have sin left, and you will have conscience left.

What else will you have left when you get rid of the Bible? You will have *death* left. The Bible does not make death. The Bible tells us about death. So you may get rid of the Bible but you will still have to face the solemn fact of death. Now, how dark it all is without the Bible! Take the Bible away, and how utterly bedarkened the world is when you come to the fact of death.

Men have groped and have speculated and have guessed and have wondered, without the Bible, whether there can be anything beyond the grave. Plato and Socrates, mighty scholars who lived before Jesus came, in the presence of death said: "For aught we know, that is all." And Caesar stood up in the Roman senate and speaking of death said: "For all we can tell death is the end of all." Now, if you get rid of the Bible you will be utterly in the dark concerning the fact of death.

When Death had triumphed over Jesus on the cross, and that body was laid in Joseph's new tomb, I can fancy Death stalking like a conqueror in that garden, as he looked on the tomb in which Jesus' body was sealed. I can fancy Death, that fearful monarch of the long centuries, saying: "I am victor over every field." I can fancy Death saying: "I brought Adam to the grave. And I brought Methuselah and Noah and Abraham and Moses and David and all the children of men to the grave. And now, behold, I have brought Jesus to the grave." I can fancy Death, as he stalked in that garden, saying: "I am victor." But on the third day Jesus in that new tomb pushed aside the door, and came out victor over death. You take the Bible away and you know none of that. You take the Bible away and the grave is a grim sarcasm that ends all. You take the Bible away and we bid goodby once and forever to our loved ones when they leave us. The Bible tells about death.

What else? You can get rid of the Bible, but you won't get rid of the fact of a *life beyond death*. The Bible does not make immortality. The Bible talks about immortality. The Bible does not make heaven and hell. The Bible talks about those two places. You may get rid of the Bible but heaven and hell and eternity remain.

You may get rid of the Bible then, if you will, just like this young king did of old. What have you left? You have God left, and you must answer to Him. You have sin left, and you must have deliverance from it, or it will destroy you forever. You have conscience left, and it will utter its cry of protest and remorse, soon or late. You will have death left. You will have an after-world beyond death left, whatever you may do with the Bible.

Oh, you do not want to get rid of the Bible. There is nobody here who wants to get rid of the Bible. What do you want to do? You want to walk in its light. You do not want to take these faithful admonitions of God, holy and good, gracious and merciful — you do not want to take this scroll, the Word of God, and cut it to pieces by neglect, by indifference, by resistance, and fling it all into the fire and say: "I don't know anything about it." You do not want to pursue that course. Sane men and women, hurrying through time into eternity, you want to face the facts, and you want to adjust your life in the way that shall be wise and sane and safe forever. You want to come with all your need and waste and loss and failure and sin to that great Saviour Jesus, who came down from heaven and died for us all, and now waits to have our consent that He may be our Saviour.

How simple it all is, and how glorious! Do you say, "I am here with bitter memories; I am scorched by fiery temptations; I am scarred by many a failure, many a defeat; I am here, having missed the right road for a long while"? Never mind. Jesus is sufficient. Jesus is able. Jesus is mighty. Jesus will save you, if you will surrender to Him. Will you? Oh, to be for Jesus! How glorious beyond words to be for Jesus with all your heart and mind and soul!

In one of the great expositions, in the art gallery two pictures were hung side by side. One picture was called "Waiting for the Verdict." It was a marvelously expressive picture. In it there was a woman, a wife, helplessly wringing her hands. About her were some little children, pulling at their mother, staring into her face, with mute and awful agony. And there was an old grandmother, holding the baby of this wife in her arms. The look on the grandmother's face was likewise pathetic beyond human speech. Beyond this group was a door slightly open, and within could be seen a man sitting in the prisoner's dock, waiting for the verdict. He was on trial for his life. That was the first picture, "Waiting for the Verdict."

And beside it was another picture, entitled: "Acquitted." Oh, how different was the second picture. The woman had her arms about her husband's neck, and her head rested against his heart. Joy was pictured on her face and on his, and the faces of the children were wreathed in smiles indescribably beautiful. The old grandmother was lifting the baby girl up to kiss her acquitted father.

See the two pictures. What is the verdict now in your case? Condemnation, separation from God, loss of heaven, loss of eternal life, the waste of your life here, and then its lasting, unceasing, eternal waste beyond the grave? That is your portion if you are not for Christ. But if you are for Christ, though your sins be as scarlet, and though your memory is painful, and though your conscience stabs you with cruelest and most poignant stabs, if you will yield to Christ, He will forgive all. He will cleanse you and make you free. Oh, yield to Christ, the Divine Saviour. Let Him be your Saviour. If you will pray this prayer: "God be merciful to me a sinner," and mean it, He will save you, because he says: "Him that cometh to me I will in no wise cast out."

It is this Book that brings you this good news of salvation through Jesus Christ.

CHAPTER VII

Need for Encouragement

CHAPTER VII

Need for Encouragement

~~~~~~

*Yet now be strong, O Zerubbabel,
saith the Lord; and be strong, O
Joshua, son of Josedech, the high
priest; and be strong all ye people of
the land, saith the Lord, and work;
for I am with you, saith the Lord of
hosts:*
*According to the word that I cove-
nanted with you when ye came out of
Egypt, so my spirit remaineth among
you; fear ye not.*

HAGGAI 2:4-5

EVERYBODY should be an encourager, and no-
body should at any time be a discourager. In times of vast
changes and upheavals and unrest and perplexity, such as
these through which the world is now passing, we should all
be doubly diligent to give encouragement in every way
possible to every person possible, and to every good cause.
Everybody needs encouragement, from the eager, growing
child in the home, to the restless boy and girl in the school,
to the young man and maiden in the college, and on to all
groups and ages and conditions of men and women. Everybody needs encouragement in the strenuous battle of life.

Those little words: "I believe in you" or "I am for you"
and "Never mind difficulties, I believe you can win and
you will," are words of untold meaning to men and women,
as they journey with life's loads and with its duties.

That is a touching story they tell us about President Taft
when he was Governor-general in the Philippines. His
health was somewhat below par; his spirit was down accord-
ingly; he was far away from his home and cherished friends

89

and fellowworkers. He tells us a group of his trusted comrades and classmates of Yale were having a dinner in the homeland and thought of him and sent him a cablegram which said: "Bill, old fellow, we are all thinking of you tonight; we all miss you and love you. We want you to know that we are for you to the end of the journey." That was a little thing for those men to do, but Mr. Taft said, "I was back on my feet in one minute, after I got that cablegram." Everybody needs encouragement, everybody needs reinforcement, and it should be the habit of our lives to give encouragement in every way we can to everybody we can.

One of the best ways of all to encourage people is by our words. Words are living things, words do things, words make their way into human minds and hearts; and often far more than men need money or material gifts they need the right word from us. The lame man, we are told in the Bible, was laid at the gate called Beautiful where he received alms when the people went to and from the temple. There he was, the poor beggar, asking for alms from all who came and went; and when Peter and John came by, his hand was stretched out for alms from them. Simon Peter said: "Silver and gold have I none; but such as I have give I thee; In the name of Jesus Christ of Nazareth rise up and walk." And the man rose up and leaped for joy and praised God. Was not this more valuable than money, a whole bank of money? What a tremendous thing! Everybody should make it a point to say the right word to as many people as he can as often as he can. Everybody should be an encourager.

This behavior of Simon Peter is a pattern of what we should be and say and do. The Bible calls our attention to different challenging examples of men who did the right thing. You think of old Caleb. What a grand man he was! Caleb was the type of man needed today. He was needed yesterday. He will be needed when we pass on and others succeed us.

The prophet Haggai knew how to give encouragement to the people. In an hour of awful distress and defalcation on their part, a time of neglect and defeat, he said:

Yet now be strong, O Zerubbabel, and be strong, O Joshua, and be strong, all ye people of the land, saith the Lord, and work: for I am with you, saith the Lord of hosts, according to the word that I covenanted with you when ye came out of Egypt, so my spirit remaineth among you. Fear ye not.

The prophet, I think, was an old man when he employed these words. What an inspiring sight to see an old man or woman marching along toward the sunset hour, courageous, grandly faithful, without murmuring or complaining or bitterness; faithful in word and deed, faithfully journeying on toward the end. Often one such man or woman saves a whole situation from disaster.

I have been on boards of various kinds from my youth, and I have seen them in a panic and I have seen one brave soul say words that in two minutes clarified the air, changed the whole atmosphere, and turned a threat of defeat into a shout of victory.

This story is in the book of Haggai which has only two chapters, and it is both vital and interesting. I suggest that you read the book today and note the occasion of these words spoken by the prophet Haggai. It was a time of great neglect upon the part of the people as to the Lord's work. Such times come, alas, again and again. The people had left aside God's work for the most part, and they were building themselves fine houses and elegant homes while the house of the Lord lay in waste and ruin.

The temple needed to be rebuilt and they were not rebuilding it. Haggai spoke these great words to the people in a time of neglect of their spiritual duties. This fine old man was summoning them to leave their selfishness and the lower things of life and to give primacy to the supreme

91

things. Satan had greatly tempted them away from the highest. He is always at work. He is ever alertly busy. I have not heard of his taking a vacation at any time, this wretched enemy of men, Satan. He is always at work. He was at work in Hagagi's time and he is at work today. And as the prophet explains: "He has all of you men and women off the track and you are following his devices instead of the Lord's counsel, and disaster is ahead for all of you." The prophet summoned them to the holy task of rebuilding the temple, no longer to allow the house of God to lie in waste and shame and ruin.

Satan is ever busy at his destructive work, never constructive, never creative, always down-dragging, always inervating, always down-pulling. That is the spirit of Satan. We are to hedge against his wiles, everyone of us, all the time. A man said to me recently that a certain man in one minute gave him the blues. Well, that certain man did not have the right to give his comrade the blues. We are to find ways to speak creatively, constructively, inspiringly, and we are to be able like Caleb or Haggai, to show the people the way out and up, from the valley of discouragement to the mountain-top of hope and victory.

As you read the story today in Haggai, you will find that Satan employed two ways to drag the people down. He is like a chameleon; he will change at any minute to carry his point. Sometimes he becomes blustering; he roars like a lion and would scare us half to death, if he could. And if that does not work, he comes like an angel of light, seeking if possible to deceive the very elect of God. Paul says, "We are not ignorant of his devices." We sane men and women, Christian men and women in particular to whom I speak for the moment, we are not to be ignorant of Satan's devices. We are to be on guard against them.

Satan employed two methods here to deceive the people. First he tempted them with false counsel, saying: "You have to take care of yourself first. Of course the temple ought to be built, but not now; build your own fine houses first. Get that all attended to and then you will have plenty of time to rebuild the ruined temple." That was Satan's first attack, and it is a very pleasing, powerful attack, for we are selfish creatures by nature, often expressing our nature in wretched behavior. Satan knows that people are naturally selfish.

Selfishness, how wretched a thing it is! The parent of all sin is selfishness. So Satan said: "Build you nice houses. You can look after the temple later; there is plenty of time. Build you nice houses." He sought to make the people selfish and he is all along seeking to do that. So Satan's counsel was: "You and your children, your wife and all of you, are entitled to have a lovely house, with nice furniture, beautiful mirrors and all the rest. Look after that first."

And then his second attack was: "You do not have to hurry anyhow. There is time enough to build that house of worship. Although the temple of God lies in waste and ruin and is mocked, spat upon in contempt by everybody who sees it, there is plenty of time."

I think that is the master trick of Satan. That is his master trick especially with lost men. "There is plenty of time" and he knows they may die at any moment. I have preached to men within this church and have seen their faces turn the palor of death, and then later along they have died in a moment, in a twinkling of an eye, before the supreme matter of their soul's salvation was settled. They said: "There is time enough yet, tomorrow, after a while." That is Satan's supreme scheme of destruction. So, he said to those people of Jerusalem in Haggai's time: "Look after yourselves first, now while you can. Fix things up for yourselves. Then take care of the house of God. You do not have to hurry anyhow. You have plenty of time."

All down the years, that has been one of Satan's masterpieces. There was never a good work proposed that there was not somebody to say: "Not now, by and by, after awhile. That is all right, very good, but this is not the time."

93

Perhaps you recall that old leader, Ethelred, who was never ready for any forward movement, never. That old Saxon king was always for a thing, but always said: "this is not the time. I am for it, you understand. Do not misunderstand me. I am for it, but this is not the time." That was Ethelred, and he went down in history characterized as "Ethelred, the unready man." We are to be ready men and women, prompt, unhesitating, whenever the call comes and unabashed by whatever the toils and difficulties are that may be involved in the call.

In that hour the prophet Haggai stood forth and made his call: "Oh, Zerubbabel be strong, and be strong Joshua, and be strong all ye people and get to work, and every one of you get to work, and if you will, 'My spirit, saith the Lord, will go along with you, just as I covenanted with My people when I brought them out of Egypt. I have not removed My spirit; I have not changed My purpose. I will be with My people, if they will be with Me and go on; and they need not fear, no matter what they may face.'"

That is the word the world needs now. That is the word all of us need. Lay all that wrong talk aside and get to work, to the right work, to the major work, to the God-given work, and do not let self have dominion over you, but let Christ utterly dominate you.

Yes, that is the right word. Haggai said it to all the people. Let the high priest get to work; let the governor get to work; let all the tribes, high and low, old and young, get to work, and everything will clear up and the situation will be better and victory will come. It is a great story, a wonderful story. It is filled with lessons. I have time to magnify only two for a moment.

First of all, God prohibits discouragement. He forbids it everywhere in the Bible. God condemns discouragement. We see all along the undoing power it has, just as was the case when those spies came back from Canaan and made their wretched, pessimistic report. They kept the people of Israel out of Canaan for forty long years. Ten of them said: "The country cannot be taken. There are walled cities over there. The men are giants and we are as grasshoppers in our own sight, and in their sight."

But Caleb and Joshua made a minority report and said: "There are walled cities and the men are giants, and there are difficulties many, but we are well able to overcome with God's help." But the ten won out against the two and the awful distress of forty years followed in the wake of their wretchedly pessimistic report. God condemned them for their discouragement.

Discouragement can come to us in many ways. For one thing, Christians are called to walk and live and serve in the realm of faith. We are to walk by faith, not by sight. In the world we see and hear, there are banners flying, there are trumpets sounding, there are great groups marching, there are pictures on the screen, there are all kinds of visible, outward tokens. The kingdom of God does not come in that fashion. The kingdom of God cometh not by observation. The mightiest forces in the world are the silent forces. My very soul is hurt when Christians forget that, and when they think they have to adopt the ways and the fashions and the methods of the world. Christians sometimes do that.

You remember that ancient incident when "God was not in the earthquake, God was not in the fire and God was not in the wind, but God was in the still small voice." That still small voice is mightier than all the armies in all the earth, mightier than the earthquakes and the tempests and the fires and the winds. God's people are to remember that the kingdom of God cometh not by observation.

"We walk by faith, not by sight" is a Christian saying which might well be emblazoned over the entrance to every church of the Lord Jesus Christ. The world walks by sight. "You must show me," they say. "Let us see your figures; let us see the tabulation. Put it on the blackboard." Oh, the kingdom of God does not come that way. If a church should have one little boy saved in a year and nobody else should be saved, that one little boy might be a Spurgeon or a Broadus or a Carroll, or a Luther or a Livingstone who may change the world. Our mathematics are very different from God's mathematics. We are to walk by faith and not by sight. In the kingdom of God victory is guaranteed by Spirit rather than by numbers.

Then again we are tempted to be discouraged because of the endless difficulties that confront us. As soon as we get through one difficulty, there is another. We can work out one problem and say, "Now I will rest awhile," but before we can rest, another problem bigger than the first comes up. But that is the way of life. We are not here to loll and luxuriate on flowery beds of ease. That is not what we are here for. "Wage a good warfare." "Put on the whole armor of God that ye may be able to withstand in the evil day, and, having done all, to stand." Haggai said, "Get to work," quit your idleness and get to the work, to the main work, the highest, the supreme work.

We are intimidated and appalled by difficulties. If we take things as they appear in the world today, I tell you our heads will hang down. It looks as though the whole world is in peril of war. At any moment a match may touch it off anywhere. That is the way it seems, and perhaps that is the way it will be. But there is one factor we must never lose sight of and it is the main factor. There is "God within the shadows keeping watch above His own." God lives and loves and cares and reigns in righteousness. Every vainglorious, godless and selfish leader in the world shall ultimately be dethroned and cast into the pit of destruction; for Almighty God hath decreed it.

The victory will not be Satan's but Christ's, of whom it was said: "He must reign, until he hath put all enemies under his feet." It is a predestined necessity that the Lord Christ must reign. Every babel of iniquity on the earth shall go down. Every selfish leader in the world shall be unhorsed and cast from his throne. Christ cares and lives and loves. He says to us: "In the world ye have tribulations: but be of good cheer; I have overcome the world."

You remember when Carey the shoe-cobbler talked and talked about going out into the world and telling the pagan world about Jesus, they laughed at him. "He has wheels in his head," they said. "He is a fanatic, he is off balance." Then a man of great influence rose up, disgusted with young William Carey and said: "Sit down, young man, sit down. When the Lord gets ready to convert the heathen He will do it without your help or mine." That was fatalism, a doctrine which still has considerable sway, teaching that God is responsible for it all and taking away our sense of responsibility.

In a letter from a missionary in war-torn, bludgeoned, starving China, a missionary out there for nearly forty years wrote: "I do not know what will come next. Some of the soldiers have been around our compound and have watched us; they examined and looked and peered. I do not know what will come next, but I am not afraid. My time is in God's hands and 'I will lay me down in peace and sleep, for our Lord maketh me to dwell in safety.'"

Certainly there is no safety in all the world for anybody in the world, apart from God. There is no safety for anybody not complying with and in obedience to the will of God. "Keep on following me and I will give you victory." That is the message of God. He forbids and prohibits discouragement and He graciously imparts encouragement.

Through the prophet Haggai God assured the people that if they would do His bidding and give His cause first place, then springs of life-giving water would break forth for them in the dry places. His power and strength and blessing would be upon them. Yea, their material needs would be met, for said He: "The silver is mine, and the gold is mine."

97

And what God said to His people of old, He says to His people now. His message to the people by Haggai is a message for us today.

Men of God, with God's help, can do anything in the world that God asks them to do. But friends, there will be failure and defeat and disaster if men leave God out. God says: "Obey my will and I will be with you. I will cause the heavens, the earth, the sea and the land to work for you. I will turn the desire of the nations towards this my house which shall be filled with my glory; and in this place will I give peace, saith the Lord of hosts."

Do you know who that "desire of all nations" is? The desire of all nations is Jesus, the one only adequate helper, unfailing and infinite in His resources. And He would say to us: "Give me the primacy, the preeminence in your lives, and do what I bid you. Do it whether it is dark or bright, whether you see signs of triumph or whether it looks as dark as midnight; just go on and do what I tell you, and I will bring you off more than conqueror and you will be amazed at the trophies of triumph which will crown your days and ways, if you do what I bid you."

In these discordant days, in these nervous, restless, frightened days, Christians should draw nearer to Christ, talk the right talk, live the right life, and render the right service.

We are on trial now; we are being tested now. Oh I am prodded with questions every week by men of unbelief who say, "Do you think you are getting anywhere with Christianity?" My answer is, "Assuredly yes. I know we are. Christ, not Satan, will have the ultimate victory." These are times of awful testing, of fiery trials for Christianity; Christ will have the field. Ultimately all His enemies will be cast into the pit, and every God-despising influence shall be brought to destruction in its own torment.

Now you and I are to keep right on saying, "I cannot see; I cannot forecast, but I can love and I can trust and I can obey and I can give my best and that is what I am going to give. I am going to give Him my best, of thought, of loyalty, of love, of service, of life. I am going to give Christ my best to the end of the day, until the sunset hour and the nightfall. I am going to give Christ my best." Surely that is the word for us as Christians. That would be my word to you if it were the last word I had to say.

Is there somebody here today who says, "I have been discouraged and cast down and undone, but I turn to Christ, the one adequate Helper and Saviour, even now; I know He can and will help me and give me the victory"? Yes, Christ will do that and much more for you.

Does somebody say, "I never came out for Christ but I ought to have done so; today I will be for Him; today I will give Him my best; today I dedicate my life, I yield my all to Christ and He will forgive me, cleanse me, save me, renew me, empower me, and take charge of me"? My friends, He says, "I seek not yours, but you." He wants you, the man, the woman, the boy or the girl. Say to Him, "Here, Lord, I give myself to Thee, that Thou mayest cleanse me, forgive me, renew me, empower me, guide me and use me."

Who comes bravely forward saying, "I link my life with Christ's church today, gladly." As we sing together now, who comes?

CHAPTER VIII

Count Your Blessings

CHAPTER VIII

Count Your Blessings

~~~~~~

Thou hast granted me life and favor, and Thy visitation hath preserved my spirit.

—JOB 10:12

IT IS of vast importance that every one of us should stop often and recount God's blessings and mercies to us. That little song, "Count Your Blessings" has in it much merit, certainly so far as the thought is concerned:

When upon life's billows you are tempest-tossed,
When you are discouraged, thinking all is lost,
Count your many blessings, name them one by one,
And it will surprise you what the Lord has done.

It is of vast importance that we give ourselves often to the blessed task of enumerating our many mercies, and we shall find that these blessings come to us faster than we can count them. Ingratitude toward man and toward God is a sin most heinous. You have indicted a man severely when you say about him that he does not have any sense of gratitude. You have indicted him terribly when in truth you can say of a man that he is ungrateful. Ingratitude is unmanly when it is toward man, and ingratitude is treason when it is against God.

One of the most blessed of all the exercises to which we can give ourselves in the world is that exercise of calling to mind every day the kindness and mercy of God toward us and ours. That hymn that we have sung from childhood is so appropriate: "Come Thou Fount of Every Blessing."

> *Come thou fount of every blessing,*
> *Tune my heart to sing Thy grace;*
> *Streams of mercy, never ceasing,*
> *Call for songs of highest praise.*

We should especially see to it that we find occasion for thinking of our blessings when the dark and cloudy days come, for one of the ways to drive those clouds away is to recall the days of sunshine and mercy and blessing.

The man who spoke this text was in the cloudiest day of his life. To all appearances there was neither sun nor moon or stars in the whole horizon of his life. Job had lost his property; he had lost his children; he had lost his friends, for they were fair weather friends. Finally, when the terrible physical distresses came upon him, those fair weather friends deserted him; and it would even seem that his own wife had turned atheist, for she said to him: "Curse God, and die!"

But Job, even in that terrible time, had his colloquy with God. Was there ever another such conversation as this man had with God? If you want your heart to burn, go and read that chapter in Job where he talked with God. Note Job's humility and his penitence, note his straightforwardness and then his gratitude, as right out of the depths of that sea of trouble into which he had been plunged, he cried: "Thou has granted me life and favor, and Thy visitation hath preserved my spirit!" What a wonderful recognition of God's mercies in such a day as that!

Job here mentions three things for which profoundest gratitude should be given by us all.

> *Thou hast granted me life, Thou hast granted me favor, and Thy visitation hath preserved my spirit.*

He singles out three truths, and these three truths are so commanding, so wonderful, that they should make every soul, even out of the deepest sea of trouble, look to God and bless Him. O may we do just that this Lord's Day evening.

First of all, Job said, "Thou hast granted me *life*. I am yet alive. All has been taken from me, it would seem, except life. But, as long as I have life, I will worship God, its Giver, and I will honor God, its Author, and I will bless God, its Sustainer. Thou hast granted me life!" Does not your heart kindle this evening at the thought that you are alive, that you are a human being? Oh, the abnormality of the man who wishes to get away from life! Do you ever read Keats? How weak is much of his poetry! As you read it you will find lines like this:

> *I am half in love with easeful death!*

That idea runs through much of his verse. Great it is to live; great it is to be a human being. Do you not feel tonight the deepest thankfulness that God made you a human being? What if He had made you a tree? What if He had made you a rock? What if He had made you a bird, or some beast of the field, or the dog there on the porch, or the serpent there in the grass? Oh, what reverence, what humility and what thankfulness should be in our hearts because God has made us human beings and clothed us with potential dominion over all the world about us!

Read tonight that eighth Psalm, which says: "When I consider the heavens, the work of Thy fingers, the moon and the stars, which Thou hast ordained; what is man, that Thou art mindful of him? And the son of man, that Thou visitest him? For Thou hast made him a little lower than the angels, and hast crowned him with glory and honor. Thou madest him to have dominion over the works of Thy hands." What a wonderful thing it is to be a human being; what a great thing is life!

What a story it would be if we could come up here one by one and recount the perils out of which we have been delivered! There was that great train wreck; but you were spared, and so was I. There was that automobile crash; but you were spared, and so was I, while others went down to

105

dusty death. There was that awful peril at sea; but you were spared, and so was I. There was that scourge of the "flu" and other sicknesses, when men and women fell round us every day; but you were spared, and so was I. How our hearts ought to be lifted in adoring, wondering and grateful praise to such a God as is our God! He spared us despite the fact that we are sinners.

I asked a man not long ago why he was cutting down a tree that grew in his yard. He said, "Because its limbs are dead and withered and fruit has ceased to grow on its branches. What do I want with a non-productive and worthless tree?" And the man cut the tree away. The man said, "This tree is no longer useful to me, it is not profitable, it is not serviceable; I will be rid of it." And the man destroyed the tree. Yet you and I have been spared, and with all that we have often forgotten our Maker and have played the part of the ingrate.

Oh, the wonder of it! God not only gives us this life, this bodily life, but He gives us life eternal. "He that believeth in Me, though he were dead, yet shall he live, and he that liveth and believeth in Me shall never die!" Oh, the wonder of the life that never dies! I was talking this evening with a friend as we drove to the bed sides of several sick ones, and he remarked to me: "How wonderful it is that God gives eternal life to those who trust Christ!" Eternal life; not life for today, not life for a doubtful length of time; but eternal life. Christ says, "My sheep hear my voice and I know them, and they follow me and I give unto them eternal life." Trust God, and you shall never perish. How wonderful is life!

You shall hear some day that the preacher before you is dead. Oh, no! His tongue will be quiet, his pulse will be still, his heart will have ceased its beating, but he will be alive — more alive than he is now, more alive than he has ever been in this world! He will have gone from this life;

106

he will be where the conditions of life are perfect, because God gives those who trust Him eternal life.

And Job also said: "Thou has granted me *favor*." God's favor is expressed in so many ways! We could talk for hours about the mercies of God to the children of men. We will consider some of them. God has given you a good, sound body. Is not that a cause for which to be devoutly thankful? Sound bodies — well bodies. There may be some about you who are blind, but you are not blind. What deep cause for you to praise God and be thankful to Him that your sight has not been taken away! How thankful you and I should be that we can talk, that we can hear, that we are not crippled or maimed! Where has gratitude gone? Have we been turned into brutish beasts that we cannot thank God for our health and strength of body?

And then, you have a sound mind. How grateful we should be that our minds are unclouded! Ever and anon some mind will reel, and reason on its throne will stagger, and one whose mind was once joyful and bright will become clouded, because reason has fled and the mind is a blank. If you would see sights and hear sounds which you can never forget, spend two or three hours in an insane asylum. You will wish for many a day you had not gone to carry away those sights and sounds on your mind and heart. But you have your mind, you have your intellect, you can think and reason, you can put this and that together logically and go your way. What cause you have for thankfulness to God!

You have your road in life, you have your daily tasks, you have your living, you have your income, you have your comfortable sense of competence, you have your job, you are able to work and you have work to do, you have a sufficient amount coming in as the product of your work, as the wages of your work, to keep the wolf from the door and make you and your family comfortable. How wonderful is the kindness and mercy of God to you! Perhaps you are very successful, your business is growing and expanding day by day,

107

your savings are increasing steadily, and every atom of it is because of the mercy of God! If He were to withhold His mercies from you for one moment, your health would be gone, your mind would totter and your reason would fail you. But for God's favor, your business would disappear like the mists of the morning.

"Thou hast granted me life and favor, and thy visitation hath preserved my spirit!" God *visits* men. How? Does He visit them as of old? How many times He has visited you, how many times has He paused at the door, even at the very door of your heart! Jesus said: "Behold, I stand at the door and knock: if any man hear my voice and open the door, I will come in to him, and will sup with him, and he with me." God visits men. How? In many ways. He visits them spiritually. There are men and women in this house who could tell of God's visits to them spiritually.

I was a child of ten or eleven years when the sense of sin was first borne in upon me, borne in upon me so strongly that I feared to fall asleep at night in the little country home. I had sinned and knew it. I was wrong with God and knew it. Some have felt the conviction of sin more than others. Some have had their hearts fairly torn to shreds, so terrible, so deep was their conviction of sin. Oh, the power of the conviction of sin, the tragedy of the heart that is exposed before God and trembles out of its personal sense of sin and separation from God and utter helplessness before the onslaughts of sin!

Perhaps in the quietness of your room it was there settled with you, and you said, "Christ is mine and I am His." Or in the church, in the great congregation, while the preacher preached and prayers were offered for you, the light came to you, and you said, "I see it! I see it! At last I see it! Never can I save myself. I am a sinner separated from God, already condemned, and I cannot save myself, but Christ can save me. I surrender to Him, and confess Him, here and now!" How wonderful that hour of conversion!

108

If I may take the liberty of making a personal reference, I will say a word about my own conversion. I was converted when I was about nineteen years of age. There, before my friends from childhood in the little country church I confessed: "I am for Christ. I accept Him. I yield to Him." As I went out of the little church house that night, all the way down the road the very trees seemed to me to be clapping their hands, and the very heavens seemed to be putting on new expressions of joy.

Christ is the Savior of sinners. All through the earthly life Christ visits us and gives His angels charge over us. He comes Himself; He never leaves us, never forgets us. He will be with us in the dark and cloudy days, just as He was with Job and Paul and all the others of His trusting friends. He will be with us when the shadows are about the home. He will be with us in all the upheavals and losses and disappointments that come as men and women travel the road of earthly life — at every step He will be with us, leading us on.

God has given you life; God has given you favor, favor in body, favor in mind, favor in soul. Your Saviour offers not only to be with you here, not only to save you here, not only to glorify life here, but He offers to be your Pilot when you leave this life behind and embark upon the boundless sea so that you will be carried safely home. Christ offers you eternal life if you will trust utterly in Him and surrender completely to Him. Have you made that surrender? How many here can say, "I have made my surrender to Christ; I have taken Him as my Saviour"? Oh, that is a great company!

Here and there in this press of people this summer night some hands could not be lifted. Some could not say, "I am at peace with God." Is there some one here in this press who says: "I want to be right with God; I want to be saved; I want to have forgiveness of my sins; I want to have life eternal"? There are some uplifted hands that say, "I am not right with God, but I would be right." Are there not others? Yes, I see yours — and yours — and yours — and yours — and yours. There is a hand lifted in the balcony. You are saying, "I want to be right with God." Are there others here to my right? I see yours — I see yours. Does another hand rise in the balcony? Is there anyone on this side of me who says, "I would be right with Him"? Does your hand lift? Does your hand in the balcony lift? Now yours — and yours.

O soul, soul! Satan does not care that tonight it is in your heart to come, if only you will defer action about coming to Christ! Satan does not care, if only you will delay making your surrender to Christ! Come now, I charge you, I pray you, I summon you! Christ's time is today. Say to Him now, "If ever I am to be saved, Christ must be my Saviour." Make your surrender to Him now. Perhaps it is already settled with you. Come, then, and give me your hand if you will make honest surrender to Christ. Let those come who say, "I have made my surrender, and I want to take my place in the church with God's people." Come now and give your hand while we sing our hymn of invitation:

> *Jesus is tenderly calling thee home —*
> *Calling today, calling today;*
> *Why from the sunshine of love wilt thou roam*
> *Farther and farther away?*
> *Jesus is calling the weary to rest —*
> *Calling today, calling today;*
> *Bring him thy burden and thou shalt be blest*
> *He will not turn thee away.*

CHAPTER IX

The Sin of Omission

CHAPTER IX

The Sin of Omission

~~~~~~

> *As the Lord commanded Moses his servant, so did Moses command Joshua, and so did Joshua; he left nothing undone of all the Lord commanded Moses.*
>
> JOSHUA 11:15

ONE of the most challenging lives in all the Bible is that of Joshua, the successor of Moses. Here is a revealing sentence paying high tribute to that remarkable man. It is given in the eleventh chapter of Joshua:

> *Joshua left nothing undone of all that the Lord commanded Moses.*

You will agree that this is a remarkable sentence: "Joshua left nothing undone of all that the Lord commanded Moses," the immediate predecessor of Joshua.

None of us ever know for what God is getting us ready. Joshua did not know in all the disciplining and training and daily experience he had in his early years that he was being prepared to be the successor of Moses, the mightiest man of the Old Testament. When God disclosed to Joshua that he was to receive the mantle from the passing Moses, Joshua was utterly overwhelmed. He demurred; he pleaded inability; he shrank with unspeakable trembling. God came to him with these great words: "Be of good courage; as I have been with Moses, so will I be with thee. Fear not, faint not, fail not."

David did not know when he tended the sheep that God was getting him ready to be the king of the great kingdom of Israel. Elisha did not know when he followed the plow that God was getting him ready to be the worthy successor of Elijah. Paul did not reckon upon the greatness of his world mission when God had him in seclusion three years in Arabia. We do not know and often have no idea for what God is getting us ready.

All down the years outstanding lives have appeared, and the world has been made larger because of their service. Do you suppose that the little Welsh boy, David Lloyd George, had any idea as a growing child in Wales, as an orphan lad, that in the most critical hour in the life of the British Empire, he was to be her Prime Minister, steering her through one of the stormiest, most desolating wars in all her history?

Do you suppose that the rail-splitter, Abraham Lincoln, had any dream in those days of crude early living, that one day he was to be President of these United States, and was to wield an influence which would go on and on with ever accelerating momentum and greatness through coming generations?

Joshua's life vividly teaches the truth that promotion comes by way of faithfulness. If a man will not be faithful in the little things, he will not be faithful in the great things. If he is careless in the smaller details of life, he will be careless when he grapples with the big issues of life. Faithfulness in the least means promotion to the much. Promotion comes by the way of faithfulness.

The whole Bible magnifies that truth. It stands out with remarkable clarity in the parable of the talents. One man was given five talents, another two and another one. The five-talent man doubled his five and received a great reward. The two-talent man took his talents and doubled them and he received exactly the same reward as was given the five-talent man. If the one-talent man had been faithful with his one talent, he would have been rewarded identically with the five-talent man or the two-talent man. Promotion is based on faithfulness.

114

This story of Joshua reminds us that there is no difference in disobedience from action and in disobedience from inaction, which is another way of saying that the sins of omission are just as real, just as grave, just as reprehensible as are the sins of commission. The sin of the people of Meroz was one of omission. "Curse ye Meroz, bitterly, because they came not to the help of the Lord, to the help of the Lord against the mighty." The people of Edom were cursed for the sin of omission. They were unpatriotic, inactive, non-cooperative in a day when their country was swept by great peril.

Jesus brings out all this with much vividness and effectiveness when He reminds us, "Inasmuch as ye did it not unto one of the least of these, ye did it not unto me." How terrible is the condemnation which Christ put upon the sin of omission!

Now Joshua, our text reminds us, was not guilty of the sin of omission. Joshua left nothing undone of all that Moses had been commanded by the Lord to do. He took up the work of the conquest of Canaan, and the people obeyed him as they had obeyed Moses. "He left nothing undone of all that the Lord commanded Moses." Is not that a high tribute to Joshua? Not many men are willing to carry out plans made for other men even though they be God's plans. This incident is profoundly suggestive to every one of us today.

Let us now look for some of the great lessons of this story. First of all is the lesson standing out here that it is easy to leave undone things of great moment which ought to be done. We sometimes congratulate ourselves on the things we get done. Now it behooves us earnestly to inquire: "What things have I left undone that ought to be done? What duties have I overlooked? What responsibilities have I neglected? What privileges have I disregarded? What sins of omission have I committed?" If all of our sins of omission were to stand out vividly before us, I dare say that our hearts would be dismayed and confused.

One of our great leaders a little while ago, when he looked back on the year that had just closed, said, "The things that trouble me most this last day of the old year are my sins of omission." You and I could say the same thing time and time again. The thing that troubles us is the thing left undone, the responsibility passed by, the privilege offered but disregarded, the sin of omission. It behooves us in all the realms of life to look faithfully and search diligently and check up on ourselves to see that the sins of omission do not dominate our lives.

Especially do we need to look at our bearing, our attitude toward the three divinely appointed institutions which God has given mankind for their betterment. He has given three great institutions for the highest good of human society, the home, the state, the church. They are all divinely given institutions. The first God-given institution for the betterment and happiness of human society was the home. The home — the citadel for both church and state. As goes the home, so goes the state and so shall go all else throughout the social order. The right kind of homes mean the right kind of social order. The wrong kind of home means confusion, consternation and defeat.

We should check up on ourselves concerning this first institution that God has given us. What is our attitude, our bearing, our relation to our homes? Are our homes what they ought to be? Are they what God wants them to be? The welfare of us individually and of human society around us depends upon our homes. What about our homes? Do the right standards prevail there? Are they maintained with scrupulous fidelity?

I have had occasion to say, and I keep on saying, that I am more concerned about the American home than I am concerned about any one thing on this earth. If the home be dedicated to the highest, then church and state and all else shall be prospered. What if the home shall allow its banners to droop, its standards to fall, its ideals to go down into the dust? Then all else will be imperilled.

Every member in the home has his or her part to play. Parents have their place of supreme responsibility and privilege, and the children likewise have a place of high responsibility and privilege. How beautiful ought to be the fellowship between parents and children. How comradely and understandingly ought to be the relation between the father and his son, between mother and her daughter! The highest things need to be stressed continually before the whole household. The highest things, the chiefest things need to be exalted always in the home.

The husband and the wife in their relation each to the other — how considerate, how faithful, how careful these relations ought to be! By neglect, by the sin of omission, by forgetfulness or inattention, by giving emphasis to other things rather than the chief things that make for the glory and perpetuity of the home, lives can be warped and hearts broken, through the sin of omission.

One calls to mind that story by the keen-minded woman, George Elliot, concerning a husband who put secondary things first, who neglected the chief things which make home-life gracious, beautiful, holy, and blessed. He rose early and toiled late and gave little attention, little consideration to his wife until it was too late. The husband was set on getting property and more property and still more until one evening when he came home, his wife, Milly, was at death's door and in a few brief hours had passed away and the big business man was stirred as out of some ghastly nightmare. The wife of his heart, the mother of his children was now cold in death and he was dumbfounded and utterly overborne. Speechless was he in the presence of his overwhelming bereavement. They carried the body out to a quiet place, and after the grave had been covered over with flowers, and the people had gone, the husband threw him-

117

self across the grave and wailed out his cry, "Milly! Milly! I did care for you. I loved you more than all else. Do you hear me now, dear?" No, she could not hear him now for he had waited too long. The sin of omission is a tragic sin!

In the home, the little things, the delicate things, the gracious things, the beautiful things need to be done by us all seven days in the week. The home life is America's great problem now. You are not to have standards there which will turn your children's feet downward. You are not to have habits there which will make their awful imprint on the young lives so plastic and responsive. You are to exalt ideals and standards in the home that will conserve life at its highest for those coming after you down through the years.

There is another institution divinely given, namely, the state. Civil government is by divine appointment. "The powers that be are ordained of God." The state is divinely given. The affairs of the state are to be orderly and worthily administered. Intelligent cooperation, nobly expressive of the right kind of serviceableness should be given. Every member of human society is a part of this civil government and every member owes a high duty to civil government. That means that we are to vote. That means that we are to render our taxes as they ought to be rendered and then pay the taxes without reserve. That means that our best thought ought to be given to the affairs of civil government. That means that time and patience and co-operative service ought to be given by us all to the affairs of civil government.

Who needs to take part in this great matter? All of us. The pulpit has its great function. The pulpit, as I understand, is not ever to turn to partisan, personal, rancorous, political discussions. The true preacher is as much concerned for the welfare of the men of one political party as he is for the men of another political party. He is never to descend into personal, partisan politics. The preacher is all along to enunciate certain principles. He is to remind the people that "it is righteousness that exalteth a nation and that sin is a reproach to any people"; that if they build on the shifting sands, they shall in time be overborne. He is to remind the people that anything anywhere in the social order that corrupts, that enervates, that cheapens, or pulls down is the thing to which the state ought not to yield. All along, the people are to lay this great function to heart. All classes, the men and women, the teachers, the bankers, the physicians, the lawyers, the farmers, all the people have a high responsibility in this great matter of conserving civil government for the highest and best. None of us are to assume a defeatist attitude and say, "What can we do about it?" When governmental affairs are rotten and evil, we are to do something about it.

We are not to give ourselves to terrible denunciation, unpatriotic speeches, but we are to give ourselves positively to thought, to prayer, to patient service, that the wrong things in the social order may be expelled therefrom, and that the right things in the social order may be builded on worthy and wise foundations. We ought to be concerned about the laws fashioned by the legislators; and if there be wrong laws, every citizen ought to do his part to change them. Every citizen ought to be concerned about who shall represent him in the halls of legislation. If evil overtakes the state, then all of us in the social order are guilty of the awful sin of omission.

There is one other institution which I will speak of for a moment. I have spoken of our attitude toward the home, and our attitude toward civil government. Now there is the other — our attitude toward the church of our Lord. Jesus said: "On this rock I will build my church and the gates of hell shall not prevail against it." Here is an enduring and divinely appointed institution founded for the building of a better world — the church of the Living God.

119

> *I love Thy kingdom, Lord,*
> *The house of Thine abode,*
> *The church our blest Redeemer saved*
> *With His own precious blood.*
>
> *I love Thy church, O God!*
> *Her walls before Thee stand,*
> *Dear as the apple of Thine eye*
> *And graven on Thy hand.*
>
> *For her my tears shall fall*
> *For her my prayers ascend;*
> *To her my cares and toils be given,*
> *Till toils and cares shall end.*

You can make your witness, your work, your giving more effective through the church than anywhere on the face of the earth. God in his great wisdom fashioned for us the church. This one institution from the hand of our Divine Saviour and Lord, the church, should have the utmost and unceasing support of every friend of Christ.

Now our lesson is plain. We do not desire to omit placing emphasis where emphasis ought to be. We do not want the sin of omission, the sin of inaction, to enthral and betray and mislead us. If we do not guard against the plain sin of omission in the home, in civil government, in the church of God, that insidious sin will lay hold upon us and cause us to bring dishonor upon the name of Christ and His kingdom.

Let us look again to our behavior in all these relationships. If the sin of omission has been given leeway in our lives, let us repent of it and cast it from us. If any of us here today or any who are listening in are guilty of the sin of omission in home-life, in government-life, in religious-life or church-life, let us wake up to the seriousness of our condition. If Christians are listening to me now whose attitude toward the church is not co-operative but neglectful, let me beg that you make a decision to change your ways and to follow worthily your church-leadership.

Are there those here today who say: "I have never made the great choice concerning Christ; I have thought about this step; I have meditated on it again and again; I hear God in His mercy calling upon me to follow Him; today I obey His call; I will follow where He leads"?

Is this call of Christ sounding in the minds and hearts of others here who hesitate to accept His gracious invitation? Let me remind you of the fearful fact that many will miss heaven simply because of the sin of omission, their failure to accept Christ and the salvation He so freely offers. "The wages of sin is death; but the free gift of God is eternal life through Jesus Christ our Lord."

Jesus said: "Every one therefore who shall confess me before men, him will I also confess before my Father who is in heaven. But whosoever shall deny me before men, him will I also deny before my Father who is in heaven."

This "whosoever" means you, O hesitating man, woman, boy or girl. What is your answer? Will you accept and confess Him now? Come if you will!

CHAPTER X

Causing Others to Sin

C H A P T E R X

Causing Others to Sin

~~~~~~

> *Jeroboam the son of Nebat, who made Israel to sin.*
>
> —I KINGS 22:52

THE Bible has much to say about the sin of Jeroboam. Many references are made to his sin. His sin cast its shadow over the reign of fifteen of the kings of Israel. His sin was so grievous that for centuries it was consciously felt in the life of Israel.

It would seem that some men have no other mission in this world, except to be a warning. When you read the life story of Jeroboam, can you find any other reason at all why we are told about it, except that his story may be a warning? One example after another in Holy Scripture passes before us, of men who seemed to have no other mission in the world, except to be a warning. Can you imagine any other mission for Herod than that he was to warn men, perpetually, against certain courses? Can you imagine any other mission for Achan, the man in Joshua's army, who brought such destruction to his army? Can you imagine any other mission for Judas Iscariot, who sold his Lord for thirty pieces of silver? Oh, horrible mission that, for a man simply to be remembered as a warning! Such seems to have been the mission of this man Jeroboam.

Jeroboam the son of Nebat, who made Israel to sin.

I wish you would take your Bible and read all it has to say about this man as here and there references are made to him, and you will come out of such character study wiser than when you began. Many pungent lessons grow out of this story of Jeroboam, who caused Israel to sin. I may indicate some of them, with a brief word of amplification.

In the story of Jeroboam, we have the attempt of a man wholly to meet life's work and difficulties by worldly strategem. He did not invoke the help of heaven when he came to the throne. He utterly disdained to call upon God for His counsel and His wisdom and His guidance when thrust into a place of responsibility and leadership. By worldly strategem, by human wisdom, by fleshly cleverness, this man sought to carry forward the kingdom when he came to the throne. The vast cause was taken wholly into his own hands, and he sought not the counsel of God, and disdained to follow God in any way.

Here is the case of a man who attempted to pass off the counterfeit for the real. When he came to the throne he found a religious people. Mark you, I did not say Christian. There may be, and often is, an impassable gulf between religion and Christianity. All men have religion. There was never an exception. There never will be an exception. The atheist who blasphemes the name of God is a religious being, for he was made in the image of God. He is endowed with a conscience and is given the faculties of will, memory and judgment. And though he is fallen from that high position in which man was created, as all of us are, yet he is a religious being, and the religious element in him may be appealed to without hesitation and with confidence.

Although Jeroboam when he came to the throne found a religious people over whom he was to rule, yet Jeroboam did not mean at all to recognize the worship of the true God. The worship of the true God meant rigid living. The worship of the true God meant the cutting off of sin. The worship of the true God meant death to selfishness. The worship of the true God meant to treat men correctly and rightly. It meant worship and work after a most righteous and diligent fashion, and this man meant to go in no such way. Finding as he did a religious people, he saw that he must deal with that situation, so he sought to divert the people from the worship of God to the worship of idols.

The record points out how he made two images and set them up, the one in one section of the land and the other in the other section, and then said to the people: "It is too difficult for you to go up to Jerusalem to worship; that is asking too much; religion should be an easy thing. There should be no hardship about it; there should be no restraint, no self-denial, no taxing difficulty, no strenuous labor, nothing rigid. I have brought religion to your own doors; I have made the image of God for you, and you do not have to take a long journey to Jerusalem there to worship God, but you may worship right here." You may see how stealthily Jeroboam thus turned away the true worship of the people of God.

This man's character and conduct is the revelation of a case where a man distinctly abused the privileges and lessons of that divine providence by which he had been elevated to a great position. It was God who brought Jeroboam to his elevated position. The difficulties in the way of his reaching that place were removed by Almighty God, and God distinctly and definitely brought Jeroboam to his exalted place. Though he was put there by the Almighty, just as soon as he mounted the throne, without any delay at all, the king sought ways and means whereby he might utterly ignore God, and turn the people away from Him.

That fact leads to the suggestion that any man who is given success, who uses such success wrongly, will be brought to ruin. There is not an exception in the world's history. Let a man be given success, leadership, prominence among men, and let him selfishly and wrongfully use that success, let him divert it from high and holy aims, let him turn it into channels sordid and selfish, and the day surely comes when that man will be defeated. Earnest attention needs often to be called to this truth. Let any man use his position in the world, religiously, to accomplish selfish ends, and God will see to it that such man wastes his influence and gets to the place where he cannot lead men at all. Take religious history and you will note that the men who were lifted up to some high place of responsibility, influence, and leadership, and yet trifled with it, sought to make it avail for their own glory, were selfish with the leadership wherewith they were endowed — there is not an exception where such men failed to be ultimately discredited and undone in influence and in holding their leadership over men. Instances many may be called to mind.

Napoleon, that matchless genius in the military world, that man who Gladstone said had the most marvelous brain ever packed into a human skull, that man who had a leadership over men that was amazing and unparalleled, who used that leadership for selfish ends and literally waded through blood to accomplish his purposes, even his mighty strength was all turned away from him, and yonder on the lone island of St. Helena, exiled and defeated, he died.

Let men selfishly use their success or their leadership over their fellows, and they will sooner or later be defeated. That is one of the reasons why the clever politician, applauded today, is in the ditch tomorrow. Let him forget the high claims of state and the best interests of her citizenship, and men will know it tomorrow and will cast about for some other man to lead them in the affairs of state. Any man who improperly uses the success that God has given him will come down to defeat. Surely, this is a truth that may not be over emphasized. Success is ever to be used for righteous ends, and if it be not so used, whether in religion, in society, in business, in the state, anywhere, its possessor is marked for defeat and for doom. That truth stands out with terrible significance here in the story of Jeroboam.

There is this other lesson in the story. No people should suffer themselves to be led to the relaxation of discipline in their living. Relaxation in the discipline of life inevitably leads to deterioration of character. Hear the king when he mounted the throne, as he said: "It is too much for you people to go up to Jerusalem; it is too much; the journey is too long; the labor is too much; the exegencies are too many. Let us make religion simple and easy. Instead of going to Jerusalem to worship, I will make images of God and put them right here at your gate, and it will be an easy thing for you to worship, and we shall not have that rigidity of discipline that has obtained hitherto." With the relaxation of discipline in Israel came the general deterioration of Israel's character which marked it fearfully for many generations.

That cry of Jeroboam is the cry of the demagogue. That is the cry of the insincere man. That is ever the cry of the man who does not mean to conform his life to that which is right, inflexibly right. Jeroboam said: "The end may be reached by any sort of means. There is no need for a man to be strict and conscientious and inflexible in life's work." He substituted expediency for principle, and in such substitution he marked his nation's doom and downfall. And therefore our text declares that Jeroboam made Israel to sin. Read the whole story, and in its awful phrases see how Israel sank, how Israel went from one low degree to another in forgetfulness of God, in idolatry, in debauching passion, in waste and wreck and doom of all the nobler powers of life.

Jeroboam so behaved himself as to make all Israel to sin Here we see the peril and power of influence. Oh, is there anything so stirring to a serious man's heart as the thought of the peril and the power of influence? How can any man sit down and think soberly a dozen minutes and consider how perilous and how powerful may be his influence, except with the deepest stirring of his heart? Jesus talked about that when he said: "It were better for a man that a millstone were hanged about his neck and that he be cast into the depths of the sea, than that he should cause some little one to stumble." This truth stands out here with startling significance, the peril and the power of influence.

The application of this truth may be traced on every side, in every realm of human endeavor. I wonder what men mean, who write their books and fill their papers with their contributions, when there runs through the book or through the paper some subtle, insidious poison, that, little by little, stealthily and fatally puts its virus into the very blood of the public. John Angell James, a noted Englishman, said that when he was a lad, a bad man put into his hands a pamphlet which he read in fifteen minutes, but which left its taint on his life even to the hour when he was writing, and he was then an old man. Full many a time the writer in the newspaper, in the magazine, in the tract, in the book, may write down something that will as thoroughly poison the soul as some awful poison will kill the body. What can such men mean when they themselves stop to contemplate the peril and the power of influence?

And then again, I wonder what some public men mean, careless and reckless as they are about their influence? Only a few days ago a young fellow startled me when I was trying to win him back from the awful throes of drink. I said to him, "Where on earth did you contract this ruinous habit?"

He said, "I got it by going with my superiors, my employers. We took jaunt after jaunt and went on excursion after excursion, and on those excursions the men older than I drank morning, noon and night. My employer pressed it again and again into my hands, and said, 'Boy, be not timid and shrinking; drink with us.'" Now the lad is in the awful clutches of drunkenness, even now fighting delirium tremens.

Jeroboams have broken many a mother's heart as they contributed to the ruin and damnation of young daughters. Jeroboams have taken sleep from the eyes of the fathers of many a drunken lad. Jeroboams have marked many a young man for a drunkard's grave, and a drunkard's grave means a drunkard's hell. What can Jeroboam mean to be so careless of his conduct, of his example, of his personality, of his influence, as to bring such results as these?

The significance of this Old Testament story has a bearing everywhere. Its application is in the affairs of state. Its application is in the city. Its application is in corporations and combinations of men, as well as in individual and isolated cases. Men can be so careless in the state as to fashion laws that will debauch the public conscience, and Jeroboams can make all Israel to sin with perverted and debasing laws. Men can be so careless in the management of a city's life as to fashion such statutes as will produce terrible forgetfulness of the will of God. The forgetting of God by any city will give death-dealing gangrene to that city and will sooner or later mark it for destruction. Men in position, men who guide the affairs of state, men who are in position to form and to mould public opinion and standards, are under the fearful responsibility of using their influence for the good, the uplift, the helpful guidance of others. What if they fail to do this? What if their influence is for evil rather than for good, for tearing down rather than for building up, for Satan rather than for Christ? What if by their example they are influencing others to take the downward rather than the upward way, the way that leads to hell rather than the way that leads to heaven, which is the way of Christ, who said, "I am the way, the truth, and the life. No one cometh unto the Father, but by me"?

Tragic indeed is the condition of those whose example and influence are for evil rather than for righteousness, who cause others to stumble and sin and be lost. Concerning such Jesus said, "But whoso shall cause one of these little ones that believe on me to stumble, it is profitable for him that a great millstone should be hanged about his neck, and that he should be sunk in the depth of the sea." That was Jesus' way of saying that those who cause others to sin are under the condemnation of Almighty God.

131

Fairness leads me to say that sometimes people in high positions do not realize, for the time being, what harmful effect their conduct and influence may be having on others. But fairness also leads me to say that when such harmful effect upon others is brought to the attention of a person who is essentially honest of head and heart, that one will make haste to correct the error of his wrongful way, and do all within his power to remedy the wrong that has been done. And, doubtless, he will find it needful to seek God's forgiving mercy and saving grace for himself so that he may have the strength and courage and decision of character to change from a wrong position to a position that is right in God's sight.

Let me tell you about an incident that occurred in a Texas city where I was preaching in revival services. It not only illustrates the point I have just been making but it is really a summary of the whole message of this hour.

Two young lawyers often were seen in the congregation. I became deeply interested in these young men. One morning I called upon them at their law office to confer with them about personal religion. They received me cordially. I asked them, "Why are you not openly and positively on Christ's side?"

They said, "We will give you a reason. Perhaps you will not think it a good one." Then they mentioned the name of a distinguished and influential jurist of that city whom I had known for some years. They said, "He is not a Christian, he is not a church member, and we have taken him for our model."

I said, "You have indeed chosen a splendid man. He is one of the most interesting men I know."

Then they said, "He rarely goes to church; he is a brilliant lawyer and a most useful citizen. We have concluded that if he can afford to pass personal religion by, we can afford to follow his example."

After a few words more, I left them and went straight to the judge's office and fortunately found him alone. He greeted me cordially and invited me to be seated. I said, "I need not sit down, Judge. You are busy and so am I. I have come to ask you a question in ethics."

"All right," he said, "what is your question?"

I said, "Does a man have a moral right to occupy a position, in the occupancy of which position he will hurt somebody else?"

With deep earnestness he promptly replied, "My answer is a positive no! A man has no such moral right. But what is the application of your question in ethics?"

Then I told him of my visit to the two young lawyers and what they said to me, and how they were sheltering behind him. I can never forget his agitation. He went over to the window and looked out across the city for several moments, then he came back and said, "I cannot answer that question, can I?"

I said, "Only in one way, sir."

He took me by the hand and said, "I will be at the services tonight." Without another word I left him. Day wore to nightfall, and I stood up to preach. I saw the two young lawyers in the audience. Just then the judge entered and was seated near the front. That evening I preached to one man. When the sermon was finished I gave an invitation which the judge knew included him. Promptly he arose, came forward, and grasped my hand as he said, "Your question in ethics got me this morning. As soon as you left my office, I locked the door and fell on my knees and said, 'Oh, God, has it come to this, that I am staying out of the kingdom of God myself, and by the power of my personal influence am causing others to take the downward way? Forgive me, and help me that my influence may be saved as well as my soul.'"

He had just finished saying this to me when I said, "Look, Judge, behind you," and turning, he saw the two young lawyers waiting to take my hand and his as they said, "When we saw you start, Judge, the thing was decided with us."

Oh, the power of influence for evil, or for good! Which shall it be in your case? The soul-destiny of others, as well as your own, may be determined by the answer you make. Let us pray now that your decision may be right in God's sight.

CHAPTER XI

An Essential of Victory

CHAPTER XI

An Essential of Victory

~~~~~~

Learn to do well.

—ISAIAH 1:17

ONE high conception of this life is that it is a school. All of us are pupils in the big school of life, and we have many teachers. The lessons are often exceedingly difficult, and the tests are often very trying. Everywhere we go life is a school. It is a school at the store, in the shop, on the farm, in the court house, and everywhere. Life everywhere is a school, and we are always learning, and ought to be. Now, our text is a great challenge of four little words, but big in their meaning:

Learn to do well.

These words suggest several lessons for us this morning. First, it is necessary for us to learn if we wish to know. Many definitions have been given of man. One definition given of man is: "Man is the laughing animal." A Frenchman has said: "Man is the talking animal." Rugged old Carlyle said: "Man is the tool-using animal. He knows how to use tools, and that differentiates him from the rest of creation about him." But a clever Englishman has said: "Man is the being who learns." And his definition, I think, is better than these others.

Man is the creature who learns. Man needs to learn. The other creatures about us do not seem to need to learn. They seem instinctively to know what to do. The bird that builds its first nest builds just as good a nest as the last nest which that bird will ever build. The spider that spins its first embroidery across the window does it the first time as well as he does it the last time. The bee that constructs its cell and then compounds its honey does it just as well the first time as the last time. These birds and insects of the animal world about us seem to know instinctively just what to do.

Man must learn, and must be always learning. That truth stands out everywhere. It is illustrated by all the virtues and graces and gifts of life. Take the virtue of *contentment.* That must be learned. With all the frictions and collisions and disappointments of life, if you and I are to come to that place in life where we shall have the contented mind and heart, we will have to learn it. Even the Apostle Paul had to learn it. Great as he was in heart, in mortal purpose, in intellect, Paul said, "I have learned in whatsoever state I am therein to be content." Paul had to learn the great art of contentment. And that is true of all of us.

Take the great virtue of *sincerity,* and we must all along work at it. It is easy to pose. It is so easy to be spectacular. It is so easy to go the way of affectation and of unreality. Oh, how Jesus reprobated everything that smacked of pose or affectation or unreality. A constant fear in my heart is that many people seem to think that posing and spectacular stunts are progress in the kingdom of God. Now we are to be sincere. It is a virtue that is to be learned, more and more and more, to be real, to be genuine, to be sincere.

Take the virtue of *self-control.* Certainly that is a desirable virtue. But few, if any, have it to start with. Did you ever see a perfectly self-controlled boy or girl? The grace of self-control must be learned, here a little, and there a little, more and more and more. How splendid it is! "Better is he that ruleth his spirit than he that taketh a city." Many clever people, fine people, noble hearted people, spoil every social circle they enter because they have not learned self-control. They utter the unfortunate word. They give the unfortunate look. Self-control is a lesson hard to learn and practice.

Take the grace of *speaking the truth,* acting the truth, living the truth. We must all the time watch lest we warp the truth. We are prone to exaggerate or deal carelessly with facts, and do so without evil intent. So often we allow our prejudices to give us the jaundiced eye and the discolored judgment. The grace of veracity must be learned in the difficult school of experience over which an enlightened conscience presides.

Take the grace of *hopefulness.* That grace must be cultivated constantly, the grace of hopefulness. Every man's life should radiate cheerfulness and hopefulness. A man advertises his own defeat if he goes whining and complaining through life. He makes it harder for himself and he makes it harder for everybody else to live as life ought to be lived. Every man should set himself the goal of living a brave, hopeful and cheerful life.

All that has been said about these other virtues and graces can likewise be said about that noble virtue called *patience.* Patience is one of the most needed of all virtues, and one of the hardest to learn and practice. Some of us never learn it. But it pays rich dividends to those who possess it!

All these graces are little by little and step by step to be learned. We are to keep ever at the task of learning.

The highest education of all is stated for us in our text of four words: "Learn to do well." That means learn to do well in the realms of the physical, the mental and the spiritual. There is a learning that begins with our body, and every boy and girl, and man and woman, of every age, ought to take the right care of the body. What a marvelous instrument the human body is, when it is kept as it ought to be! How clean and chaste and pure the human body ought to be, and how forceful, how vital as an asset is the human body in the big battle of life! There are men dying at fifty who ought to live to be eighty, but they burned out life's reserve forces. They burned them out by maltreating

139

the body, by making it a temple of self-indulgence, when it ought to have been kept as a holy thing for the service of God in the big battle He has for us in moral life. The body is to be looked after reverently and constantly.

And then we are to advance from the body to the mind. We are all the time to be improving the mind. Everybody ought all the time to have some worthy book, some worthy literature at hand. Toiler in the factory, man in the bank, teacher in the schoolroom, preacher in the pulpit, editor at his desk, everybody ought all the time to be studying. Some talk about reaching the deadline. A man will reach the deadline, intellectually, when he quits studying. Some lawyers and preachers say that they fear when they reach fifty or fifty-five they will have passed the deadline and be useless thereafter. They will pass the deadline and be useless, for the most part, at twenty-five, if they quit studying. But the man of sound body who continues to study and improve his mind can be as zestful and helpful and interesting at eighty as he was at forty years of age. It was that way with William E. Gladstone of England. Moses spent eighty years learning to do forty years work, and furthermore, he continued to learn throughout the last forty of his hundred and twenty years.

But the care of the body, the education of the body, is not enough. Nor is the education of the mind enough. Some of the greatest villains the earth ever saw were men superbly educated in their brains, adroit, plausible, scintillating in intellectual development and power. That is not enough. Knowledge is power, but there is something far greater than that. Character is power. The man of character, the man trustworthy, reliable, dependable, the man builded on the right foundation, the man whom the people can trust — he is the mightiest man on earth. Washington held the United States, the early colonies, in his hand, for they trusted him. There were other men about him far more learned, far more clever, far keener intellectually, but Washington was dependable. Washington was trustworthy. Washington had learned to do well. Character is power.

We are to learn to do well, and that brings us into the moral and religious realm. We are to do that which is pleasing in the sight of God. We are to learn to do that which has the approval of our great Maker, our divine Guide, our one rightful Master. We are to learn to do well, lest we take the evil road, the end of which is death. To do ill, to do wrong continually, means to end in death. There never was a wrong thing that paid, from the first wrong deed that earth ever saw until the last one committed today. Wrong is stupid. Wrong is blunder. Wrong has in it the seeds of self-defeat.

A young man in this city did one bad deed when he was a boy about eighteen. I am working now to put him on his feet. But when he goes to this place or that or the other, and they ask: "Give us your record," and in that record there stands out one dark chapter, because of which chapter he went away for several months to a federal prison, the lad comes shambling out of the office and back to me, saying, "That one dark chapter is as a millstone about my neck. I will never get over it." And it is true that he is handicapped for life.

Wrong means defeat. It means defeat for the individual. It means defeat for society. It means defeat for the state. Wrong-doing never pays. Learn to do well, to do right, to do the highest things, because in that is blessedness for the spirit. We are to learn to do well and to keep ever at that task.

Now, a second word: How are we to learn to do well? I have three words to say about that, as simply as I can say them. How are we to learn to do well? Three things are needed. We need a pattern, we need power, and we need practice. That is the simplest way I can say it. First of all, if we are to do well, we must have a correct *pattern*.

There are some who would teach us that if we are to do well we should see how ugly, how deformed, how crooked, how repulsive evil is. There are some novelists whose books reek with filth, and, alas, many of our young people are reading them. Many novelists imagine that they must bring all the ugly chapters out in their fiction if they would help the people in the highest and best way. The whole program is unsound and impracticable. There are some newspapers which rake in the filthiest gutters to get at incidents salacious and ugly in individual and social life, and spread them all out in the papers for everybody to read. There is no measuring how much harm some newspapers do by a thousand and one things they print, a thousand and one things salacious and reeking and odorous. God grant that the day may come when every newspaper will print only the news that is fit to print!

It may be too much to hope; nevertheless I dare to hope that the day will come when theaters and movies will present on their stages and screens only things which are decent, helpful and constructive. If I may believe the reports that reach my ears concerning much of their so-called entertainment, then I am forced to conclude that great millstones of guilt hang about the necks of those who are responsible for the unwholesome, unworthy and ungodly, the evil, harmful and destructive influences which these public agencies exert upon both young and old. Moving pictures constitute one of the most powerful influences for good or for evil in the modern world. Oh, that their producers would place a high value on the stewardship which is theirs! The mother who is careless about her child going to this picture show or to that play, the mother who is not alert and conscientious at that point, may wake up some day to find that filth from that picture or from that play has entered into the child's deepest heart and muddied all the waters of that child's life. To the last degree we are to have before us noble patterns, if we are to learn to do well.

142

There was an ancient king who said: "I will show the people a lesson, so that they won't drink any more," and he put before them the drunkest man he could find, and history tells us that that evening everybody in his realm got drunk.

It is unwise and untrue to say that if you show people all the ugly things they will then choose only the good and the beautiful. You might as well say that the school teacher, teaching the child how to write, should get the worst copy on earth to make a good penman out of the child. You might as well say that the teacher of art should get the most grotesque specimen of art possible, and put that before the child to teach the child how to become a great artist. It is utterly foolish, and certainly is it unscriptural, to imagine that you are to learn to do well by having before you as a pattern that which is filthy and ugly and bad.

The Word of God recommends: "Whatsoever things are true, whatsoever things are honest, whatsoever things are just, whatsoever things are pure, whatsoever things are lovely, whatsoever things are of good report, think on these things." In other words: "As a man thinketh in his heart, so is he." A young man ought never to let his eyes gaze upon the foul and bad picture, and when he finds that the book he is reading kindles within him base passions, he should instantly fling it into the fire. We are to learn to do well by keeping before us the right pattern.

Jesus is the great pattern for us. Jesus should be our model. We are to imitate Him. We should seek to walk in His steps. He is the perfect pattern. Let us look unto Jesus, the Author and the Finisher of our faith!

What else do we need beside the pattern? We need *power*. Jesus not only proposes to save us if we will trust Him as our Saviour, but Jesus proposes to put a power within us above ourselves, superhuman power, divine power that will enable us to overcome evil and do that which is good, power that will enable us to follow Him and become more and more like Him. That power enables us to grow in the grace and knowledge of our Lord and Savior Jesus Christ. Because Jesus does impart that power to His believing followers, they are truly transformed. Once they were ugly, and their habits dissolute, and their lives were like charnel houses. Now they are transformed, self-controlled, temperate, and patient. Their faces glow with goodness and their deeds are noble and unselfish. Christ is living in them, as He said He would do, if they would trust Him to be their Saviour and Lord. Power comes from Him.

What else do we need if we are to learn to do well? We need *practice*. The old saying comes in: "Practice makes perfect." There can be no substitutes for practice. We need practice, if we are to learn to do well. All along we must have practice. If the child would learn how to write he must practice. The most beautiful copy in the world will not make a penman out of a child. The child must practice. If the young man learns to be a doctor, a surgeon, he must practice. He must do. He must execute. He must act. If one learns how to be a musician there must be practice, unceasing practice. Even so, if we learn how to do well, how to live the highest life, we must work at it all the time. We must practice all the time. It is do and do and do, and never quit doing. That is how we are to learn to do well in the highest and most splendid fashion.

When Jesus came to teach us, He said, "If any man will do the will of God, he shall know of the teaching, whether it be of God." "If any man will do — if any man will do!" Men talk about doubt. Obedience to whatever law Christ gives is the solvent of every doubt in the world. The biggest skeptic that earth ever saw, if he will act up to the light God has given him, will get more and more light, and soon a sun will flood his way.

A woman of great prominence and wealth said to the minister: "Everything about your religion is as dark as death to me. What could you say to me?" He replied:

"Act as if God were, and you shall presently know that He is." And she came back a few days later, radiant with light. She had found God. Obedience solves doubt. Practice. Practice. There can be no substitutes for practice in the Christian life. Many a Christian who began well, now has spiritual dyspepsia, now has spiritual indigestion for lack of practice. A man may have the light and know the truth of God. But if he follows not the light and practices not the truth he will remain a spiritual dwarf and a moral weakling. There can be no substitute for practice.

If a man is to learn self-denial, he must practice it. If one is to learn magnanimity of soul toward everybody, he must practice it. If you are to learn kindliness, you must practice it. If you are to learn liberality, you must practice it. If a man sits down and says: "After a while, when I get much, then I am going to give much out of my possessions to the Lord's cause," the probabilities are he will go on his way a miser to the grave. If a man learns liberality, he must practice it up to the limit of his ability.

That is how we are to learn to live. We are to have the right pattern. That pattern is Jesus. We are to have power, and that power comes from Jesus. And then we are to take the light and leading that Jesus gives, and we are to act up to the last limit of it, we are to practice it to the last chapter, and then we will learn to do well, and we will be doing well.

Oh, isn't the lesson plain for us? There are two great aspects to the religious life. The one is negative and the other is positive. The negative aspect is stated in the sentence of just four words preceding our text: "Cease to do evil." Then comes the text: "Learn to do well." There is the negative aspect: "Cease to do evil." There comes in repentance. It is not simply being sorry for sin, grieving over it. "Cease fo do evil." Forsake it. Leave it. Renounce it. "Cease to do evil." That is the negative aspect. Then, "Learn to do well." You cannot have a building that will

145

stand unless you have the right kind of foundation. One of the world's great cathedrals now is sinking, and when an investigation was made recently as to the cause, it was found that one corner rested on a bad foundation. Unless we turn away from every evil way, unless we repent of all that is wrong, and build on Christ, holy and righteous, our substitute, our righteousness, life for us rests on a faulty foundation. "Cease to do evil."

Then comes the positive side: "Learn to do well." It is not enough for us to stop doing the wrong things. We must do the right things. It is not enough for us to cease to do evil. We must learn to do good. There is activity. There is positiveness. There is service. We must learn to do good. The gravest sins that the Bible speaks of are the sins of omission. "Inasmuch as ye did it not," rings out yonder at the Judgment three different times. "Inasmuch as ye did it not." The sin of omission called forth the condemnation. The fig tree was cursed for the sin of omission.

Positively and actively we are to go out and practice the right way until the day is done. It is not an easy way. It is a hard way. It will have its thorns, its rough places, its heart-breaks. But Jesus will help. He will give of His power. He will say to us: "My grace is sufficient." In Him is our hope, our strength, our victory. Therefore let us cleave to Him all the way as we keep learning to do good.

CHAPTER XII

The Spiritual Recovery of the Home

CHAPTER XII

The Spiritual Recovery of the Home

~~~~~~

> *Then Jacob said unto his household
> and to all that were with him, Put
> away the strange gods that are among
> you, and be clean, and change your
> garments: And let us arise, and go
> up to Bethel; and I will make there
> an altar unto God, who answered me
> in the day of my distress, and was
> with me in the way which I went.*
> —GENESIS 35:2, 3

THE subject for our meditation together today is
the spiritual recovery of the home. The subject is suggested
for us by these words in the thirty-fifth chapter of Genesis:

> *Then Jacob said unto his household, put away the
> strange gods that are among you and be clean and change
> your garments and let us arise and go up to Bethel and
> I will make there an altar to God who answered me in
> the day of my distress and was with me in the way which
> I went.*

God's first institution that He fashioned for the good of
human society was the home. Human society is founded to
a remarkable degree on the home. The orderly development of society follows upon the orderly development of the
home. The greatness of any land depends upon its homes.
No nation can rise any higher than its home-life. One of
the most beautiful and impressive pictures in all literature,
outside the Holy Bible, is Bobby Burn's poem, "The Cotter's
Saturday Night." Every father and mother should read it
again and again, as it portrays home life anchored to God
and bowing obediently to His will. The wise and worthy

care of the home is a matter of eternal moment. Well does one of the large classes for women in the Sunday school of this church have for its motto these words: "The Home for Christ."

We are called here to a matter far more important than the secular matters about us to which we give much serious thought and effort. Here is a matter more important than business, important as that is; a matter far more important than statecraft, important as that is; a matter of more importance than our vast system of public education, important as that is. The care of the home, the wise and worthy care of the home goes before any of the important causes I have named. Civilization to a remarkable degree is dependent upon the home. Church and state are both vitally concerned about the home-life of the people; and it must be plain to all of us that the home-life of our land is being terribly undermined and endangered today. What with the telegraph, the telephone, the daily press, the automobile, the airplane, the radio and the movies, what, with all these, shall be the outcome for the home? I repeat, the serious-minded person with eyes half open must be aware that the home-life of our land is being terribly imperiled and undermined. Urgent indeed is the summons that all of us be deeply concerned as to the homes of our nation. Whoever or whatever strikes at the home-life of the people strikes at the very heart of a worthy and stable civilization.

Here in our text Jacob had come to a crisis, a very definite crisis in the life of his own family. Such crisis hours come sooner or later to most families. Jacob waked up as one out of a terrible dream to the realization of the awful drift that had marked his own steps and the steps of his household.

Thirty years before, Jacob had fled from his brother Esau, whom he had cruelly wronged, whose birthright he had taken by fraud. He had to flee from his homeland into a far country. Goaded by conscience and tormented by fear, he fled far to the north. As night came on he laid down to sleep and took of the stones to make a pillow for his head. In his troubled sleep he had a vivid dream in which he saw a ladder reaching from earth to heaven, and on it angels were ascending and descending. And God stood above the ladder and spoke wonderful words of comfort and promise to the weary and lonely fugitive.

When Jacob awoke he was filled with fear. He said, "Surely God is in this place; and I knew it not. This is none other than the house of God, and this the gate of heaven." So he arose and took the stone that he had put under his head, and set it up as a kind of altar and poured oil on the top of it. He called the place Bethel, which means "house of God." There he made a great vow to God. If God would go with him and be with him in the way wherein he went and would take care of him, would give him food and raiment and would bring him back in safety to his father's land, then God should surely be his God and he would surely devote one tenth of all his gains unto God.

That dream and that vow unto God marked a high peak in the experience of Jacob. But he, like others since him, forgot his vow. The Bible faithfully tells us that he let at least thirty years go by before he seriously set about keeping that solemn vow made in early manhood. The troubles and evils which beset him and his family in the after years forced him to a realization of his shameful neglect of the sacred vow he had made at Bethel.

The one girl in the family, Dinah, had been betrayed and shamed. Her brothers, terribly moved by their sister's shame, sought to avenge her. On every hand feuds and bitternesses were in evidence. Jacob's family had gone far down the toboggan slide and he woke up to a realization of it as a man stirs out of some horrible dream. He realized, as the prodigal realized in the far country, the plight he was in and the plight his family was in; and in that hour a great resolve came to Jacob. In his heart he heard the voice of

151

God calling unto him to go back to Bethel, the place of vision and dedication in his early life. He resolved to go to Bethel and there renew his vows. He would amend his own ways and seek spiritual blessings for his family. Hear the appeal he made to them. He said unto them, "Arise, let us go back to Bethel, change your garments, be clean, put away the strange gods that are among you; let us go back to Bethel and I will build an altar there where God met me in the long ago, where I made a great vow which I have failed to keep. I'll go back now and build a real altar there and I want all of you to go with me." This great scene, one of the most moving scenes in all the Word of God, presents vital lessons which we will do well to consider this morning.

First, let us note the exhortation Jacob gave his family. "Arise, let us go back to Bethel, be ye clean, change your garments; put away the strange gods that are among you and let us go back to Bethel where God met me long ago, where I made Him a vow which I have neglected to keep. That vow I desire to renew at Bethel and begin even now keeping the promises I made to God in the long ago." A great exhortation! There are certain things about it that are very impressive. It was made in obedience to the command of God. God said to Jacob, "Arise, and go back to Bethel where I met thee long ago and where thou didst make a great vow to me." Jacob made this call to his family in response to the command of God.

Oh, what a great thing it is to obey the command of God. "Our wills are ours, we know not how, our wills are ours to make them Thine." Behold, to obey is better than sacrifice. Obedience to Christ — that is the governing principle in His kingdom. "Ye are my friends if ye do whatsoever I command." Our Lord and Master is Christ and His commands are to be implicitly obeyed. That was a pungent thing the immortal John Wesley said to a group of his younger fellow-workers, "The rules that I have made for you are to be *minded* by you and not *mended* by you." Now if Wesley felt it important to say that, certainly with all definiteness and positiveness Christ could say, "These commandments I announce, these principles I annunciate are to be minded by you." Whatsoever He sayeth unto you, do it!

So Jacob was obeying the command of God and he was taking his proper place as the head of the family, the high priest of the family.

Napoleon said in a critical time in the life of France, "What France needs now is good mothers." He should have added also, "and good fathers"; for good mothers and fathers are needed by every country. The father cannot abdicate his responsibility at all. If the father seeks to leave the rearing of the children to the mother, the father will be a great defaulter in the sight of the people and especially in the sight of God.

Jacob took his true place and said to his family, "Put away your strange gods; change your garments; be clean now and let us all go back to Bethel where I met God and where I made Him a great vow, which I have not kept." It was a great hour, a crisis hour in the life of this man Jacob. Go over it again. Thirty years before, that vow had been made; and it had not been kept. And troubles thick and fast had accumulated in the family of Jacob. An awful situation had developed in that family. Then it was that Jacob, the head of the family, stirred as one in a bad dream and said, "The hour has come for reparation; the hour has come for reformation; the hour has come for a decisive and radical change; let us go back to Bethel; let us seek to repair what ought to be repaired; to undo what ought to be undone; to carry out what God would have this family do." It was a great hour!

It is my deepest conviction that that is the step supremely needed now by homes throughout America. Like Jacob, we should take stock of our moral and spiritual condition, a full and faithful inventory of our homes. We parents should hold solemn and loving interviews with every member of our families and households and seek as best we can to lead them into paths of truth and righteousness, paths which in many cases would take us and them back to the Bethel of past visions and vows where may be found new experiences of God's grace and mercy and power. And especially should Christian men who are fathers accept the God-given responsibilities which are theirs as heads and priests of the family. Oh, Christian fathers, have you been careless and forgetful and unfaithful as Jacob of old was for so many years? May God enable you even now to turn over a new leaf, to go back to your Bethel, to accept your responsibility as head of the family, to renew your vows and enter upon a new life of victory.

I give it, I say, as my deepest conviction that the supreme need for America today is to look again with all diligence and carefulness and conscientiousness to the home-life of the people. The father who can sleep easily with his boy trifling with the drink cup; oh, he needs to be aroused by the arousing power of God. The mother who can be calm and quiet with her daughter adopting habits that are leading toward an ill-ordered life, that mother needs to come back to her Bethel and look again at the deep meaning of parenthood and the responsibilities connected therewith. We need to go back to Bethel. Every home in this country should have a fresh inventory of its true status in the sight of God and if there are strange gods in our homes, if there are standards in our homes which would make us blush if Jesus should visit our homes, oh, if we have anything that would bring the blush of shame and humiliation to our cheeks by the visible presence of Jesus among us, let us clean it out, let us change our garments, let us put away our strange gods, let us go back in truth to Bethel and meet God. This is the great need of America today, in my humble judgment.

A nation is revealed by its home-life and no nation will rise any higher than the home-life of its people. If the home-life of the people be marked by bad standards, by doubtful practices, by low conduct, then the whole social order is involved to an awful degree, because we are bound together in the bundle of life. This man Jacob gave the right exhortation to his family. Every parent should say with Jacob, "Let us go back to that great crisis hour when we once vitally and mightily dealt with God and where in that holy place we vowed a great vow and registered a great resolve of soul, which we have forgotten to an awful degree. We should go back to our Bethel, the place of vision and of high resolve."

Notice again what Jacob said, "I am going back to Bethel and build a real altar of God there after these long thirty years." Let that resolve become personal with you and me. What about our altars unto God? What about the vows we made back yonder? What about the vow we made when the loved one was dreadfully ill and we went away into the secret place and poured out our prayer to God and made our vows? What about those vows? What about the promise you made when suddenly you faced a great crisis and all you could exclaim was, "Oh, God! Oh, dear God, help me! Oh, God, if you will help me, I promise I will do so and so"? Have you kept that promise?

What did you do with the vow about church attendance? Everybody ought to go to church. This applies especially to men and women who say they are Christians. What did you do with that vow about prayer meeting attendance and about Bible study in the Bible school? What have you done with that resolve you made: "I'm going to try my best to win souls for Christ, weak and frail though I am"? Have you forgotten that Christ gave soul-winning first place in His command to His followers?

Are your personal altars still standing? Let us look at some of these altars. What about the altar of secret prayer?

155

How much do you pray in secret? Did you pray today when the morning light broke in upon you with all its freshness and beauty? Then later, as you came to the house of God, did you pray in secret? For whom and what did you pray? What about the altar of secret prayer? What has become of it? Jesus said, "But thou, when thou prayest, enter into thy closet, and when thou hast shut thy door, pray to thy Father which is in secret; and thy Father which seeth in secret shall reward thee openly."

It was when Moses dared to be alone with God that God gave him the sight of that bush which burned and was not consumed. It was when Isaiah dared to be alone with God that God gave him a threefold vision that literally transformed the young prophet's life. It was when Jacob was alone with God yonder beside the brook Jabbok that he met God in a way never to be forgotten and had a blessing from God more gracious than human speech can describe. It is when you and I dare to be alone with God in the quiet place that we tell Him what we really hope for and desire and what we want to be and do before His face.

What have we done with the altar of family prayer? What if I ask now, "How many in this large throng within these walls and the larger throng listening in radio land, what have you done about the altar of family prayer? How many of you have family prayer? How many of you make it a point once a day to assemble the whole house together, children, servants if you have them, and all make humble, grateful acknowledgement unto God, the Giver of all good, for His mercy to you; and seek His guidance continuing and His favor unfailing for the unfolding days ahead? What have we done with family prayer? How can any Christian father be willing for his family to be reared, for his children to take their cue from him and to be to an awful degree molded by him, without having family prayer? What have you done about that? Some of us can testify that the blessings which came to us around the family altars in our childhood homes are more vivid and living and challenging than any of the blessings we remember from those early years. What are we doing in these days about family prayers?

Many men are listening to me now who ought to say something like this today, "Frail and infirm and unworthy as I am, the altar of family prayer shall be established in my home; and once a day for a few minutes at least we will pause and let God speak to us out of His Word and then we will speak to Him out of our deepest heart through the blessed medium of prayer." Some of you men will likely say, "Preacher, we do not have time for family prayers." And I say to you that you had better find time for communion with God daily in your home. It will be the best investment of time for you and your household that you could possibly make, provided you approach it as a blessed privilege rather than as an irksome duty. It need not take much time, just a few minutes of the day for you and yours, especially for those growing children. Try it! I believe that you and your family will soon come to regard those minutes as the best of the day.

What have you done about the altar of church prayer? Oh, the decline if we allow the altar of church prayer to break down, to be indefinite and uncertain. The early churches gave primacy to prayer and the whole Roman Empire was shaken to its foundations because they did just that. And any church that will give the primacy to prayer today will be visited with the merciful visitations and favor of God and the people round about will say of such church, "We perceive of a truth that God is with these people."

Let us go back and set up the altar, that altar of secret prayer. Nobody can do your praying for you, my brother, nobody but you can do that. Let us set up the altar of family prayer. Let us summon the children around us and say, "My dear children, I ought to have done this before, but I have been timid about it. I do not feel that I am anywhere near a saint, but I want you to forgive me for my

157

neglect, my dereliction and share with me now sympathetically and cooperatively as we set up a family altar to God from whom all blessings flow."

Let us magnify the altar of church prayer. Think of a deacon being absent from prayer meeting, unless hindered providentially. Think of a Sunday School teacher being absent from the appointed hour of prayer, when heart-felt pleas are made unto God in behalf of so many needy people and causes which are dear to the heart of God. Do not forget that prayer changes things. Prayer is the greatest power available to mortals. It can move the arm of God Almighty.

Take one more look at Jacob's return to Bethel. He frankly stated the case to his family and said, "Will you go back with me?" Under that brave proposal the whole turbulent and worldly group went back with their father. When a man acts honestly, humbly and faithfully, when a man is true to his Lord, marvelous results are sure to follow. The whole family went back with him. What else? When they went, the terror of the Lord was on all the cities through which they passed and the men of those cities did not follow after them to pursue them. When a man's ways please the Lord He maketh even his enemies to be at peace with them. "No weapon that is formed against thee shall prosper; and every tongue which rises against thee in judgment thou shalt condemn. This is the heritage of the servants of the Lord, and their righteousness is of Me, saith the Lord." At last, Jacob retraced his steps after long neglect and his family was recovered and great blessings came to Jacob and his family during the after years.

Surely the lesson is plain. Will we heed it? Will we heed it without delay? Oh, if it were the last word I had to say to my people and to my friends and to a needy world I would speak to you about your homes. Focus your best of head and heart on your homes today and through all the tomorrows! Why not begin even now by registering your high and holy decision for Christ and His Church?

Who tells us today, "I would like to link my life with this church, coming by letter, or coming upon statement, having you send and get my letter"? Or who says, "I would like today to make my surrender to Christ who alone can save and who hath said, 'Him that cometh to me I will in no wise cast out'; I would like today to yield my life to this unforgetting and divine helper, Jesus, who died on the cross for sinners and therefore, died for me; for I am well aware, poignantly aware, that I am a sinner in the sight of God; I want this divine Redeemer to be mine; I want this atoning Saviour to be mine and I yield my life to Him today; I begin a new life with Him; I make my surrender to Him; I receive Him to be my Saviour"? Who has heretofore made that surrender and now wants to link his or her life with this church? Come! Come now; and may God bless you in the coming!

CHAPTER XIII

The Great Woman
(*A Mother's Day Sermon*)

CHAPTER XIII

The Great Woman (*A Mother's Day Sermon*)

~~~~~~

> *And she said unto her husband, Behold now, I perceive that this is an holy man of God, which passeth by us continually. Let us make a little chamber, I pray thee, on the wall; and let us set for him there a bed, and a table, and a stool, and a candlestick: and it shall be, when he cometh to us, that he shall turn in thither.*
> —II KINGS 4:9, 10

MOTHER'S Day has come to be one of the most appealing and impressive days in the life of the American people. Today from the President in the White House to the humblest tenant in his cabin, people pause as they should do to pay tribute, grateful and loving, to the best-loved person in all the world, even a mother. The most beautiful sight in all this world is the picture of a mother with a baby in her arms. It is not any wonder that artists, painters, sculptors, poets and orators have summoned themselves with all their resources, to portray that picture in a worthy fashion.

When Jesus was dying on His cross, He paused there in the midst of His agony and revealed His love and care for His blessed mother. When Isaiah, the great prophet, thought of God, he also thought of his mother and said, "As one whom his mother comforteth, so the Lord comforteth His people." When President Garfield was inaugurated as President, it is not surprising that the splendid man, when he had taken the oath of office and had kissed the Bible, turned immediately and kissed his mother, to the delight of the watching thousands around him.

I will pause here a moment to read a brief poem written by a greatly gifted woman in our own city, Mrs. Grace Noll Crowell, which appeared in this morning's newspaper:

There Still Are Mothers

In the stress and tumult of the world today
*   We grow confused — then hope lifts like a light:*
There still are mothers — mothers who can pray,
*   Who kneel beside a window ledge at night*
To speak to One beyond the farthest stars,
*   As they commit all mankind to His care,*
For no true mother in her praying bars
*   Another's sons and daughters from her prayer.*

So long as there are mothers who thus kneel;
*   Who make God's Word a pathway, men may grope*
And wander in a maze, the world may reel
*   Beneath the shock of war, but there is hope;*
The brightest hope, when mothers pray, then wait
*   In faith that God will answer, soon or late.*

On a day like this, every one of us should find some way to voice afresh his gratitude to God for his mother. If she be still living, see her if you can and if you can not see her, send her a letter, breathing with gratitude and love, and send her the token that she ought to have from the child she has borne. If the dear mother has passed within the veil, as many of our mothers have, rededicate yourself to the high ideals and standards that she upheld, draw nearer than ever today to your mother's Saviour and Lord, and let it be a "Mother's Day" of recommitment and rededication to the highest things in life.

You may find it in your heart to make an offering to some great and good cause. One of our men, who would not allow me to call his name, sent a worthy check to me for a great cause fostered by this church and said, "This is in memory of my mother." She was one of the most honored members this church has ever had. She was truly "a saint in Israel."

Let us not allow the day to pass and the time to be consumed by little nothings. Let us rather make it count in vivid tokens, in expressions of appreciation, in prayers, in rededications which shall make for the enlargement of our own lives and the betterment of other lives. In other years we have thought here again and again about the Shunammite mother who was called a great woman. I am urged to speak on it again. Some ministers speak on it every year when Mother's Day comes. Perhaps we shall find renewed inspiration as we think again today of why the Shunammite mother was called a great woman.

If the friends here and those in radio land will read again this story of the mother who in the Bible was called a great woman, you will agree that it is one of the most impressive you have ever read. No one, nor all the stories you could name, can excel it in beauty. The glistening stars at night, the gorgeous sunset, the towering mountains, the song of the birds in the happy springtime, the laughter of little children — none of these make a more beautifully impressive theme than the story of the Shunammite woman.

The Bible is very careful in the use of adjectives. It does not waste time on improper eulogies on anybody. It does not give applause anywhere that ought not to be given. That is one of the evidences of the divine authorship and divine integrity of the Bible. Coleridge said, "The reason I believe this book is God's book is that it finds me as does no other book that I have ever read." It is God's talking book. "When thou awakest, it shall talk with thee."

We do not have to go to the dictionary to get definitions of greatness for this woman, but to this beautiful, idyllic, wonderful story. And as we read this story, there flash out three scenes in it which reveal three outstanding characteristics in the life of this Shunammite mother.

The first scene portrays her practical helpfulness. The next scene portrays her beautiful contentment with her modest lot in life. The third and climactic scene portrays her triumphant faith in God.

Let us look first at her practical helpfulness to needy humanity. Just here I think women far excel men; they perceive more quickly human need and know when and where and how to relieve it far better than do men. So was it with this Shunammite woman. When she beheld God's prophet, Elisha, in company with his servant Gehazi, going up and down the land on the prophet's mission, she said to her husband, "I perceive that this is a holy man of God, coming and going this way often. Let us add something to his comfort; let us build a little room here, the prophet's chamber, and put therein a bed and a table and a stool and a candlestick, and let it be the prophet's room; then when he and Gehazi, his servant, come this way, they can turn in and rest." That is the origin of the oft-quoted expression, "The prophet's chamber." Some of us who are privileged to be preachers have occupied that chamber in homes palacial and in homes humble, many times.

And so it came to pass that Elisha and his servant turned in to that home. The prophet was very grateful and he told his servant, Gehazi, to call the Shunammite woman to come to him. She was called and came to the prophet's door. He said, "How can we requite thee for all thy goodness to us? Would you like for me to speak to the king that your husband may have a place in the king's cabinet or palace or to the commanding general, the head of the army?"

Those were days when prophets moved among kings and in the armies, and I doubt not that if the right kind of prophets would move among kings and in the armies today, we would have better times. So he said, "What can be done to requite you for your kindness?" "Oh," she said, "we dwell among our own people; we are plain people; we are not fitted to be in kings' palaces, nor to move in army circles. I dwell among my own people. If I can be of any service in the world it is among my own people."

When she had departed, Elisha said to Gehazi, "What can be done for her?" And the servant replied, "She has no child." So he called her again, and promised her that she should have a child, and in due time a child was born and grew to boyhood. She adored the boy and she gave her best to him, and to his training. A joy forever to her was that lad. What is more beautiful than a conscientious mother bringing up her child in the way of the Lord?

I delight to recall the story of a personal experience of the president of Wellesley, that great school for women, just outside greater Boston. This gifted woman educator went down every Monday afternoon to the poorer section of Boston and there in a hall talked to the women of that neighborhood. She hoped to help those women to be happy and useful in their humble spheres of life. One very bad afternoon, when the weather was fiercely cold and the elements were all forbidding and she wanted to be at home with the doors shut and the fire graciously burning, she reasoned with herself, "I think I will not go this afternoon. Nobody will come. But I have been teaching those women that we must keep our engagements, rain or shine, cold or hot, dark or bright; consequently, I must practice my preaching." So she decided to go to the place of meeting. "Maybe two or three will come anyway, and it would be bad if I were not there."

When she arrived, lo, the hall was more crowded than ever. She was amazed and voiced her amazement. She said, "I was sorely tempted to stay in this afternoon, and probably would have, but for my insistence that everybody should always keep their engagements, cost what it may. Now, I am here without any message for you. I had not thought about my talk. I just came so that you might know I was keeping my engagement. I wonder what I should talk about?"

And one of the humble women, garbed in the plainest of clothing said to her, "Tell us please, if you can, how women in our plight can be happy."

With poverty, gaunt and pitiful, limitations wretched and terrible, what could she tell them? That fine, cultured woman said, "Why, you have given me my text; I will tell you." And she told them three things. She said, "Memorize something beautiful every day, preferably out of the Bible, for it is the best of all literature. Memorize something beautiful, a whole chapter if you can, or one verse; the Twenty-third Psalm, or one verse of it, and meditate on it.

"Then, every day, look for something beautiful; maybe it will be a little flower; maybe it will be a bird that will light on your window-sill; maybe it will be a passing cloud with a rainbow on it; look for something beautiful." And then she said, "Especially every day make it a point to help somebody outside of yourself."

That remarkable woman said that within six months that part of Boston was transformed. Those women had gone out and had done those very things. They had memorized each day some beautiful passage, preferably from the Word of God. They had looked for something beautiful. One woman said in reporting, "I could not see anything beautiful. The day was so black and stormy, so I picked up my baby and looked at her beautiful blue eyes." Then they had been helpful to somebody else every day.

The second characteristic of the Shunammite was her beautiful contentment with her modest lot in life. The prophet said, "This woman must be compensated for this beautiful kindness to us in providing 'the prophet's chamber.'" He asked her, "May I secure your husband a place in the king's palace, or some prominent place in the army?" and she demurred immediately, and said, "I dwell among my own people. Here was I reared; here must I live. If I can do anything of value, it will be right here." One won-

168

ders how many women today would have responded as did this woman.

I am thinking of a man who came to this city some years ago. I had known him back in the village, when he and I were young men. I knew his modesty. I knew about his small, growing business. I used to see him as he came to the church in the earlier days of my preaching. He rolled the baby buggy with two little fellows in it up to the church and minded them as we had our service there in the village. Prosperity came to him and in time he moved to the city where his children grew up. One day he said to me, "The saddest day I ever saw was when I came to the city. Back in the village, we all went to church. Back in the village were the happy days when I rolled my children in the baby carriage to the church; but when we came to the city, my family went seven days in the week for all that was frivolous and foolish and futile. The saddest day I ever saw," he said, "was the day I came to the city."

Oh, that men and women would put first things first! This great woman in the Bible put first things first. "Oh, no," she said, "if I can be of any service in the world, my place is here among my own people. Neither the palace nor the army is the place for my husband and me." Contentment with her lot! Contentment is a duty enjoined most earnestly in the Word of God. The lack of contentment has its hurt in every direction.

"A merry heart doeth good like a medicine." A merry heart is a medicine. A doctor said to me, "If I could break the spell of this man's melancholia, I think he would get well. But he thinks all the world has gone to destruction and he dwells morbidly on that, day and night." The Scripture says, "Rejoice evermore." While contentment helps us, lack of contentment not only hurts us and hurts others, but it hurts the cause of our Lord. The Lord's cause calls for brightness, triumph, victory. When the angel announced the coming of Jesus, he said, "Behold, I bring you glad tidings of great joy, which shall be to all people." The refrain of the angels was, "Glory to God in the highest." Christianity is harmed much if men are long faced and morbid and sour and bitter and blue and miserable. "Rejoice always." You and I have no right to unload our ugly tempers on anybody around us. Everybody has enough to bear. They have loads of their own to carry. They have secrets within of great weight and concern and we have no right to add to their troubles by our discontent and unhappiness.

A great Presbyterian preacher in New York told his people of an incident which he said had changed his life helpfully. He said he was riding on the subway in New York on one of the bleakest, most physically uncomfortable days he had ever seen, and that every time anybody got on or off that subway car, the door would creak distressingly on its hinges. He said there sat by him a plain working man, who kept looking at that creaky door. The man finally said, "I believe I can fix that," and he took from his inner pocket a little oil can, and went to the door and poured oil on those creaky hinges, and the noise was stopped. Everyone of us ought to carry an oil can; we ought not to go away from home without an oil can; we ought to have it with us all the time. There are creaky doors everywhere we go. Everybody needs the oil of human kindness. There is no place in the economy of God for grumbling, complaining, pessimistic, discordant men and women. The world is not helped by them.

We can learn how to be contented. Paul said, "I have learned in whatsoever state I am, therein to be content," or, in other words, "to be master of the situation." There is an old saying with much philosophy in it: "Make the best of it." Certainly, make the best of it.

I recall a story told by Mark Twain. A dog had howled miserably all night long where he was boarding, and the next morning at the breakfast table, everyone poured out his complaints about the dog. Mark Twain said, "Oh, let's talk about something pleasant; the poor dog has troubles of his own." That is the way to turn it. Make the best of everything.

Some terrible tragedy in life may have completely warped life from its normal way. Make the best of it. Let Helen Keller, that wonderful woman who made a beautiful life in spite of so many handicaps, help you to learn in whatsoever state you are, therein to be content. Make the best of it. Remember what Paul said, "Our light affliction, which is but for a moment, worketh for us a far more exceeding and eternal weight of glory." Just trust in the Lord and remember that He will turn it all into triumph, if we will trust Him and go on.

Now that is the second characteristic of the Shunammite woman — contentment. We can learn contentment. There are two ways to learn it. We can try to be moderate in our desires, concerning food and raiment, and for the many desirable comforts of life. If we are not able to afford them, then we will do without them. Have moderation, have simplicity in your living. The other way to learn contentment is to accept the inevitable, the unavoidable. Just say, "Lord, I turn it over to Thee; work it out your way. I will trust Thee whatever comes."

The third characteristic of this great woman was her triumphant faith in God. The child of promise was her hope, her joy and satisfaction. Motherhood, the highest glory of womanhood, had come to her. The child was a comfort to her while growing into boyhood, and then was carried away by sudden illness. She laid him on the bed of the prophet and got upon her beast and hurried on the journey to the prophet. He saw her coming and sent his servant asking, "Is it well with thee? It is well with thy husband? Is it well with thy child?" and she answered sublimely, "It is well." She had reached him at last and her arms were about his feet; she was overborne; she could not talk; she was overwhelmed. Gehazi came to take her

171

away but the prophet said, "Leave her alone. She is heart-
broken; she will tell us what it is." Then she explained her
grief to him and the prophet told his servant, "Go and lay
my staff on the boy, on the dead boy's body." He did so and
was on his way back when he met the prophet and the
Shunammite mother to whom he said, "The boy still is
silent." Elisha went to the dead boy, and life was given
back in response to the prophet's prayer, and he gave the lad
to his mother. It is easy to imagine the joy that was brought
to that Shunammite home by God's prophet.

The home is the crowning institution. It is essentially a
woman's contribution. It is woman's greatest contribution to
civilization and to Christianity. The country will go to
pieces without good homes. The churches will be undone
and defeated and will fail without good homes.

In thinking of the building of a better America, some say
economic conditions should change and some say political
conditions should change and some say educational conditions should change, and I think there should be great
changes in all these directions, but the supreme need of all
is the building of the right kind of homes in America. Then
the battle shall be "turned back from the gate." Oh, ye
mothers and ye fathers too, conjoined in your work, build the
right kind of homes! I pause for a moment on that. The
prophet asked, "Is it well with thee, is it well with thy husband, is it well with the child?" and the woman with sublime,
unwavering faith said, "It is well," although the boy was
up on the prophet's bed, quiet in death.

I press that question for a moment before we go on. Is it
well with thee, oh mother, is it well with thee? Are you
living a life that a mother ought to live? Is it well with thee,
oh father, oh husband? Are you helping that Christian
wife who is trying to climb the heavenly steps, and are you
helping the children upward with her? Are you indifferent
and non-cooperative? Oh man, you can do better than
that! For your sake, and for your family's sake and for

humanity's sake and for Christ's sake, be the right kind of husband and father!

"Is it well with thee," young people, as you begin to build your home? "Is it well with thee," older people, as you hasten toward the sunset hour? "Is it well with thee," eager boys and girls? It is not well no matter what you have nor how you are surrounded nor what you are planning for, it is not well nor can it be well if you are not trustfully anchored to Christ as your Saviour. "Let Him have His way with thee, let Him have His way with thee."

Have you not waited long enough to make the great decision, to give your glad surrender and say "Yes" to Christ? "Let Him have His way with thee." Who says, "I am now ready for Christ to have His way with me; I surrender to Him"? Come, confess Him on this Mother's Day. Who says, "I have made that surrender and I want to link my life with the church, I want today and forever to be with Christ's people"? Come as we sing: "Let Him have His way with thee."

CHAPTER XIV

The Value of Life's Unrealized Purposes

CHAPTER XIV

The Value of Life's Unrealized Purposes

~~~~~~

> *And the Lord said unto David, Where-*
> *as it was in thine heart to build an*
> *house unto my name, thou didst well*
> *that it was in thine heart. Nevertheless*
> *thou shalt not build the house; but*
> *thy son that shall come forth out of*
> *thy loins, he shall build the house unto*
> *my name.*
>
> —I KINGS 8:18, 19

WE HAVE before us this morning a very vital question, namely, "What is the value of life's unrealized dreams and hopes and purposes?" A minister in his private, personal conferences with the people is often confronted with that very question. Often a person aspires and plans and dreams and prays and hopes and strives to reach a certain worthy goal and yet his dreams and purposes seem to end in defeat. What, therefore, is the value of the lofty purposes if they are not to be carried to victorious fruition?

The Bible comes to our relief at that point, as it comes to our relief with ready council for every chapter and experience in human life, for this book is different from any other book this world ever saw or shall see. It is a book divinely inspired and accredited for our good for today and for the endless tomorrow.

I am constrained again to talk to you today on that vivid and revealing incident in the life of David in his desire to build a temple for the honor of God, and yet his desire was not carried to consummation. He dreamed about it, he prepared for it, but he did not see one stone laid in place.

This text may well point our meditation upon the theme, "The value of life's unrealized purposes."

> *And the Lord said unto David, Whereas it was in thine heart to build an house unto my name, thou didst well that it was in thine heart; nevertheless, thou shalt not build the house, but thy son, Solomon, shall build the house.*

Here was a man who dreamed and planned for years and years for a very worthy thing, namely, to build a house for the honor of God's holy name, but he was not allowed to build it. Plutarch tells us that Cato in the Roman senate was sore afraid of the power of Carthage against Rome, and that Cato finished every speech with the sentence, "Carthage must be destroyed." So David here, early and late, year in and year out, had as his dominant purpose to build a house for the glory of God.

What is the value of life's unrealized dreams and hopes and purposes? The story of this incident, with the accumulating explanation that God gives in connection with it, you will find in First Kings, the eighth chapter. The incident helps us very greatly, as we seek to answer such questions wisely. May we be divinely led to find some of these lessons today.

First of all in the incident we have a picture of the incompleteness of the earthly life. The tragedy of life is not its brevity, but its incompleteness. We are called away right in the midst of our work. Not many people can say what old Simeon said, "Lord, now lettest thou thy servant depart in peace, for mine eyes have seen thy salvation." Not many can say that. We are called right in the midst of our plans, and seemingly our unfinished work.

Abraham went out from Ur of the Chaldees to receive an inheritance but he did not get one foot of the land of Canaan, except a grave in which to sleep. Jacob went out on a great quest but he died a stranger in a strange land.

Moses, mightiest man of the Old Testament, worked for long years to weld the great multitude which he led out of Egypt into a compact confederation of people. He transformed a great rabble into a vigorous nation and yet he did not enter the Promised Land. He toiled with the chosen people many long years and died before he realized in his own life that great purpose and dream.

So, here it was with David. Long and late he toiled to build a worthy temple to God, yet he died before he saw one stone laid in its place. Our tasks are never done. We are called in the midst of our unfinished work. The broken shaft is a fitting symbol of our human, earthly life.

Lord Shaftsbury was one of the greatest men of England. He devoted his energies for the relief of poor people and when he came to die, he said to his physician, "I am not afraid to die, my peace is made with God. I am ready to go, but I have no one to look after these poor women and children. I want to live." There is your great man. You can have no faith in a man's patriotism nor in his religion, if he does not care for the people and plan for their welfare, even after he is gone.

That is a touching story about the great pioneer educator, Dr. Rufus Burleson, who for nearly fifty years was president of Baylor University, at Waco. As he lay dying, he realized that he was near the end and said to his loved ones, "Lift me up once more to the window and let me see the towers of Baylor." They lifted him up and then laid him back again upon his pillow to die. It is a great thing to live on in the hearts of people or in great institutions which one has helped to build. It is a great thing!

As long as I live I shall be remembering many of the interviews I had with Dr. B. H. Carroll, the greatest personality I ever touched. Vividly do I recall the last conference we had. It was concerning the Southwestern Theological Seminary at Fort Worth, which was the crowning achievement of his life. He said, "Do not forget the seminary, which is for the training of preachers." It was the last talk we ever had. He was going fast. Just a little before his translation, he touched me gently and said, as if he had not mentioned it before, "Brother George, do not forget this seminary." And I say to you, as Dr. Carroll said to me, "Do not forget this seminary."

That other great old man, Dr. J. B. Gambrell, whose preaching and quaint philosophy of life left its mark on the people of the Southwest, as he lay dying, said to me, "I am going now. I am ready to go but it would please me much if it were God's will for me to stay on awhile longer and help you and the others carry to victorious completion the great causes that are on your hearts and mine."

Glorious! Glorious to live like that! We can have no faith in a man's patriotism nor his religion if he be not concerned not only for the welfare of the people today but for the people of the long, unfolding tomorrow. Great souls are concerned about the future as well as the present. Seldom do they feel that their tasks are fully finished in this life.

David had a great desire which became his obsession. It was his dominant passion to build a temple for his Lord. Day and night he dreamed about it, but he was not allowed to build it. There was one great reason why he was not allowed to build it. God said to him, "You have been a man of blood and you have made abundant wars and it would be incongruent for a man of blood and of war to build a great temple to the glory of God."

What an incongruity if the saloon man who had gained his money through the blood and sufferings of women and children should come around and say, "Let me build you a church" or if some gambler who had gained a fortune by prostitution and debauchery of everything high and holy, should say, "Let me build you a Christian college or hospital." What an incongruity! God said frankly to David, "It would not be fitting for a man of blood, for a man of war to build this house; nevertheless, it is well that the purpose to build it, the desire to build it, is in your heart. Your son, Solomon, shall build the house." And Solomon built that great temple, the glory of which filled the world for long centuries.

How did David react to God's decision? Did he murmur or protest? Not at all. Not a murmur, not a protest against God's revealed will. No cynicism. He said, "Very well, while I am here, I will do all I can for Solomon." And he made large and lavish preparations in gathering materials and workers for his son to build the temple for his Lord. Then David "died in a good old age, full of days and riches and honors," before one stone of the temple was laid in its place.

His was a great life. Not a perfect life; there are no perfect lives in this world. Our friends who say they are perfect are just badly mistaken, and their profession is a very great mistake. There are no perfect lives in this world, none! There is only one perfect person who ever walked the ways of men, and He came forth from the eternal Father where He had lived from the beginning of time, and He made sacrifice upon a lonely cross on Golgotha's hill, and at the end of that sacrifice, He cried out with a loud voice, "It is finished." Atonement for sinners was finished. His was the only perfect life ever lived in this world.

And now the question emerges, "What is the value of life's high purposes if we are not to see them carried to consummation? What is their value? Is there any value?" There certainly is. God said approvingly to David, "Whereas it was in thine heart to build an house unto my name, thou didst well that it was in thine heart, nevertheless, thou shalt not build the house."

Alfred Tennyson sang, "It is better to have loved and lost, than never to have loved at all." What is the value then? What is the value of these great purposes and dreams that are within our hearts which we do not carry to consummation? What was the value to David?

First of all, the value to David himself was immeasurably great. His whole life was enlarged, greatened, strengthened, magnified, glorified, by this purpose in his heart. Great purposes enlarge life. You may well despair of the man who does not dream dreams and of the young men who do not see visions. Great purposes strengthen life and glorify it. This truth partly explains the greatness and glory of the world enterprise of missions.

Lord Macaulay gives a fine explanation of why Protestantism went down in Europe some centuries ago. He reminds us that at one time France was predominantly Protestant, but he goes on to tell us, that the Protestant people lived merely for local communities. They were parochial, they were sectional, they did not look out upon a great lost world; therefore they were undernourished, they were enervated. They had no great program of evangelism; and fifty years after Martin Luther died, Protestantism had declined to an awful degree.

Lord Macaulay, not a preacher but a man with a prophet's vision said, "If those Protestant people in Europe had taken the world into their program and had gone out to conquest, as later Cary went to India, as Judson to Burma, as Yates to China, and others around the globe, we would have had a different story of Protestantism in Europe this very day. The church will shrivel and die if it does not cherish the vision of a world program for Christ."

John Wesley said the right word for every Christian when he said, "The world is our parish, every human being in the world is in our parish, every one." And this church here is responsible to the last limit of its power for the evangelization of the entire world, all races, all sections of needy humanity in the world.

To have a great purpose enlarges life. Many plain people are working at their machine shops, their laundries, their farms, or stores or banks, and they are putting their plans, their dreams, their money and their prayers into world evangelization, and life is being strengthened and enlarged within for every one of them.

An old shoemaker, when asked what he was doing said, "I am mending shoes, and praying for a conquest of the world for Christ." There was a great man. It was a great moment in the life of David, when he desired to build a house for the Lord, and the later consummation of that dream was a great blessing to untold generations.

The eloquent Dr. Chalmers said he could never bear light talk. He was one of the most eloquent men who ever talked for Christ. He could not bear light, gossipy conversation. The great man would withdraw from a circle when the conversation ceased to be uplifting, and he would go over by the window and look out on God's beautiful world. "As a man thinketh in his heart, so is he." If we think on little things, we shall be little men; if we think on big things we shall be large within. We may not have any money, but we can have large souls, lofty spirits. We can dream large dreams and in the dreaming of them life will be enriched in many ways.

David's desire to build a temple for his Lord became the dream of his life. Under God's direction, he passed on to Solomon his dream and Solomon carried that great dream of David to glorious consummation. This is a blessed truth for parents. Let us have our great dreams and great programs and let us tell our children about them and pass on to them the dream of service. The dream of the father or mother can become the dream of the son or daughter. The unfinished work of parents can be carried on by their children, and what a goal this is for the children!

Was there ever a more pathetic sight than for fine parents to have unworthy children? Oh, children of godly parents, despise not their dreams for themselves and for you! Devote your worthiest efforts to make their dreams come true!

This is a challenge for all of us! What a glorious thing for us to be bound together in the doing of a great work! I was impressed last week more deeply than I can say by a conversation with a great citizen who said, "I was ill a few months ago and they said it looked very bad for me, but I wanted to live very much." I said, "Why did you want to live?" He replied, "I wanted to live to see a certain great piece of work done." Nobly unselfish work for human good, it was. He wanted to live to see that great program brought to victorious fulfillment.

In our lesson today, the dream of the father, David, became the deed of the son, Solomon. The dream of the teacher may become the mighty deed of the pupil; the dream, the noble purpose of some worker may find its realization in some other worthy life. Many of our glorious national institutions are the dreams of the founding fathers come true. Where would church and state be in this country were it not for our forefathers who paid the price to lay the foundation for the right kind of civilization? What a debt we owe to those who have lived before us, to our own immediate parents and their forbears!

Our goodly heritage imposes a tremendous obligation upon us of this present age to pass our heritage on to those who are coming after us, fifty years from now, an hundred years from now. Let us hope they will look upon us with gratitude and not with grief, and will write a chapter of approval and not a chapter of disapproval and poignant regret because of our unworthy behavior.

We see in this great truth today, that no good work is ever lost. Somebody will carry it on. If we give our best to a good work somebody will build on our foundation, will take up the torch where we lay it down and will carry on. The scientists remind us that there is no loss of energy in the world. They talk about the conservation of energy, and they tell us that the energy expended by a worker continues to function in the world even after the worker is gone. In other words, no good thing is ever lost. Let that thought be an inspiration to every parent, every teacher, every worker!

You remember what was said about Abraham: "Abraham believed God, and it was counted unto him for righteousness." It was reckoned unto him for righteousness. He believed God. He carried on heroically. Whatever the temporary reverses or defeats may be, we are to rise resolutely above them all, trusting in God to help us carry forward the causes that are dear to His heart.

Some of us want our desires concerning noble undertakings for God and humanity to be fully realized before we lay ourselves down for that last sleep. We want to see them undergirded, fortified, stabilized and made sure for all the years to come. Such desires are commendable. We ought to link our lives with great causes. But we must trust God by leaving the final results with Him.

Young men, if you want your lives to count, identify them with great causes, not selfishly, but cooperatively, altruistically. We are to put ourselves wholeheartedly into great causes. I speak here a moment to the church family. When you put your best into your church, your best of loyalty, of prayerfulness, of devotion, of cooperative serving and living — when you put your best into your own church, you are building for the chief cause in all the world, Christ's one institution, the church, which He purchased with His own blood.

I am always distressed to see a man more enthusiastic about his lodge or his club than he is about Christ's church. Here is a place for the expenditure of the best thinking and the best living and the best giving and the best loving in all the world. Christ will make your witness and your service go further in and by and through your church than anywhere in the world.

When you business and professional men put your best into the church and say, "This shall have my best," it will please Christ, for He loves the church.

To sum it all up, we are to "take the long look." We are to plan and to build today for the long tomorrow. We are to take the noble heritage handed down to us by our parents, our teachers, our forbears, whoever they may be, and carry it on to triumph by the guidance and will of God. As I have often remarked here, we are citizens of two worlds and if we fail to live for two worlds, we commit spiritual suicide. Unless we live for the world to come it is suicide, and unless we live for the world that now is and trust obediently in the will of God, it is also suicide. Oh, we can live grandly by trusting, dreaming, hoping, striving, praying, for two worlds.

Are you trustfully anchored to Christ as your Saviour? Do you want His will done in you and in the world, which will is humanity's hope, which will is the peace for us all? Then stand forth and link your life publicly with that great Saviour.

Who says, "I have made that great personal commitment but have not confessed it"? Make your confession today! Or, do you say, "I have held back from making that surrender"? Why hold back another hour, another minute? Salvation is of the Lord. "The wages of sin is death; but the free gift of God is eternal life through Jesus Christ our Lord." Are you willing to accept that gift *now?* For this is the day of salvation. Then come now, confessing your sins, and confessing publicly your acceptance of Christ Jesus as your Saviour and Lord.

Who says, "I do accept Him and I want to link myself with the church"? Come anchoring yourself trustfully to Christ as your Saviour.

> *He leadeth me, Oh blessed thought,*
> *Oh words with heavenly comfort fraught.*